Origins of English Pub Names

A Fascinating and Informative Look
Into Their Origins and Meanings

Anthony Poulton-Smith

First published in 2018 by
Apex Publishing Ltd
12A St. John's Road, Clacton on Sea
Essex, CO15 4BP, United Kingdom
www.apexpublishing.co.uk
mail@apexpublishing.co.uk

This print edition prepared and distributed by
Andrews UK Limited
www.andrewsuk.com

The views and opinions expressed herein belong to
the author and do not necessarily reflect those of
Apex Publishing or Andrews UK Limited.

Introduction

Pub names are derived from the English language but seem to have a dialect all of their own. Cracking the codes and imagery will show a little more of the history of the place and the locality than we could ever imagine.

Although it may seem odd, the inn sign pre-dates the first recognisable inns in this country by a significant period of time. Once upon a time, every family brewed their own ale. It made sense as the water could rarely be trusted to be safe to drink and the boiling part of the brewing process effectively sterilises the liquid. In order to earn a copper or two, some settlements would offer some of the brew to travellers on the road. Such refreshment, perhaps accompanied by a hunk of bread and pottage or similar, brought much-needed revenue to the household. We are not talking about the larger communities where the main road ran straight through the village but more isolated communities.

Yet these services would have to be advertised as any well-worn path was unlikely to run past the front door. Hence, to draw attention to the home brew, a sheaf of barley would be tied to a prominent tree. The bole of a large tree with its lower branches removed would be noticeable enough. With a sheaf of barley tied at, or just above, eye level, they would be guaranteed to receive a thirsty guest or two before long. These marked and still-living trees were known as ale stakes and are easy to see as the forerunner of the modern pub sign. This is how the logical order of pub – name – sign was, in reality, quite the reverse.

In later years, landlords and owners were quick to realise the sign was the advertising hoarding of its day. Just as modern advertisers use humour and eye-catching imagery to give their product any edge over the competition, so early inns employed every trick they could think of to bring in the customers. There was one big difference, however. Today we read the name, yet literacy is a fairly modern development and our forefathers will have had to recognise the image on the sign and be able read the message it contained.

As the centuries passed a central core of pub names developed, instantly recognisable as a reference to an inn – for example the Red Lion would never be taken literally. There are also those rare, even unique, names that have a story to tell. In the following pages these pub names are listed alphabetically, with explanations. These names come from a surprising number of areas, as we shall see as we journey through a selection of pub names – some among the most common, while others are not only unique but have a story to tell.

Origins of English Pub Names

A Bit on the Side

Humour is never far away when naming public houses and here we see a name most often used for an annex or when an extension has been added to an existing pub. Such are often used to increase the area given over to dining and, once again, the name is suitable as it can also refer to condiments, sauces and other side dishes. Of course, the most common use of the phrase is to refer to a lover of a married man or woman.

Aboard Inn

A Cumbrian pub name defined in several ways, indeed even the name itself is disputed. Normally referred to as the Aboard Inn, the sign appears to show the name as the A Board Inn and the black and white squares on the tabletop clearly show the painter interpreted this as an indication of a board game being played within. Others suggest this should be a'Board, said to be a term for 'intoxicating liquor' but this has received little support. Perhaps this points to a place with board and lodgings, yet this seems unlikely. Most promising is the suggestion this invites us to 'come aboard', a likely meaning should this have been coined by a man with links to the sea.

Admiral Byng

A naval man who had his home at Wrotham Park, not far from this Potters Bar establishment. Soon after arriving here he was dragged before Royal Navy representatives to account for the failure of the Minorca campaign. He was held to blame for the debacle and shot.

Admiral Sir Lucius Curtis

Opened as the Cork and Bottle, in Southampton's Eastern Docks, it is today named after the man who was to become Admiral of the Fleet, chosen to lay the foundation stone for the tidal dock in Southampton on 12 October 1838.

Aleppo Merchant

Numerous explanations have been proposed for this pub in Carno, Powys. Among these examples of creative etymology is the idea it refers to a pudding created in the Syrian city of Aleppo. The ship depicted on the sign is the SS *Aleppo*, a steamer of the Cunard line. This can also be dismissed for that vessel launched in the early 19th century, more than two centuries after the licence was first granted to sell spirits.

The history of the place is sketchy, a fire in the 19th century destroyed valuable records which would help to explain this unique name. Yet this seems to refer to the man who worked for the Mercer's Company, John Matthews, born around the end of the 16th century. He took wool and linen from Britain and travelled to the Middle East, returning with spices, cotton and silks from his business contacts in the city of Aleppo, Syria.

By the time he came to the village of Carno, making his way to his home town of Llangollen, he was a very wealthy man indeed. It was here he met a young lady, a member of a family of farmers named Wilson. He stayed for a time but, finding farming an unrewarding occupation, turned the farmhouse into the inn, obtaining the licence in 1632. Whatever he planned to do here is not clear, he died just eight years later.

In his will he left the inn and licence to the Wilson family. It remained in their possession for a remarkable 307 years. His will survives, showing what monies and property he bequeathed to his family and includes a charitable trust which is still realising funds. Whilst John Matthews worked for the Mercer's Company, it seems the Aleppo Merchant must have had dealings outside those of his official channels for he amassed a personal wealth the equivalent of £8 million today.

Alfred Herring

At Palmers Green this takes the name of Second Lieutenant Alfred Herring, awarded the Victoria Cross for his heroism in France during the latter months of the First World War. Joining the army in 1916, he lived in the nearby family home.

Alice Lisle

At Rockwood, in Hampshire, is the sole example of a pub, or indeed anything, with the name of Lady Alice Lisle. She is remembered for being the last woman in Britain to be executed publicly.

Her story starts with the Monmouth Rebellion, a plot to overthrow the Roman Catholic James II. The plot ended following their defeat at the Battle of Sedgemoor, Somerset, in 1685. More than 1,000 of Monmouth's supporters were taken prisoner, sent to Winchester and were tried at the infamous Bloody Assizes. Many were transported, the ringleaders drawn and quartered.

Among those on trial was Alice Lisle, husband of Sir John Lisle who had left her a widow the previous year and who was one of the judges at the trial of Charles I. She was charged with harbouring two known supporters of Monmouth: Nonconformist minister John Hickes and leading figure Richard Nelthorpe. They were here just one night and all arrested next morning. Alice was certainly more of a Royalist than her husband, although her religious beliefs were likely to make her sympathetic towards the Catholics.

At her trial there was clearly more than a little concern that this woman of 68 years should stand before them. The charge of treason was levelled at all and, those found guilty, faced the same sentence – death by burning. While the jury were reluctant to find her guilty the bullying of Judge Jeffries left them no real alternative. A week later she learned her sentence of burning had been amended to beheading as befitted her position – the Stewart idea of mercy.

Amber Rooms

Among the most creative of modern pub names, this Loughborough pub occupies the site of the town's electricity works. The word 'electricity' is derived from the Greek 'elektron' which did not mean 'electricity' but 'amber', hence the pub name.

Anchor Made Forever

Not so much one name for this pub in Bristol, this really represents two names with very different origins.

When this pub was first opened, in the middle of the 18th century, it was named after the local coal mine which had the unofficial name of Made Forever. It is held this term was coined by those who first discovered this seam, generally held to be Messrs Fudge and Lewis, thinking this would bring them sufficient funds to see them 'made forever'. We have to look across the road for the Anchor, this being where the local blacksmith's forge produced ships' anchors.

Arroyo Arms

Fittingly situated near the England/Scotland border, as it recalls the role of the Border Regiment in victory over the French in the Peninsula War. The name dates back to 1811, when a combined British, Portuguese and Spanish force, under General Rowland Hill, dealt such a crushing defeat to the French, under the command of General Jean-Baptiste Girard, the latter was dismissed by Emperor Napoleon Bonaparte.

Ashen Faggot

At Northleigh, in Devon, this pub name recalls a pagan ritual. Here the 'faggot' is a bundle of sticks, used to fuel a fire or, correctly, two fires. The faggot is made from ash, purported to be the only wood which burns readily while still green, and is lit by the old fire and used to light the new fire. As the old fire dies away, representing the old year, the new fire comes to life and shows the birth of the new year.

Historically at least, this should not be seen as the change from 31 December to 1 January. From the 12th century until 1752 the Julian calendar made 25 March the start of the new year, prior to that the lengthening hours of daylight marked the start of the coming year.

Aunt Sally

Today the traditional pub game of skittles is making something of a comeback. However, the Aunt Sally is a pointer to how the game came to the pub in the first place. This game began as an outdoor attraction, at fairgrounds as well as pubs, where the image of the head of an old woman with a clay pipe would be created out of straw and cloth. It could also be seen as the origin of the coconut shy.

Many creative suggestions have been put forward to explain where all these games originated. Yet it seems the idea of throwing something at a target will have been practised ever since early man threw a spear, or even a rock, at their potential dinner.

Atmospheric Railway

The idea of an atmospheric railway is not unique to South Devon. Trial routes were tried out in Dublin and in London but the most famous is Brunel's which it was hoped would take passengers the 20 miles from Exeter to Newton Abbot at up to 70mph.

The idea is ridiculously simple. Rather than have the pump on the rails, which is effectively what a steam engine is, position several large pumps along the length of track to evacuate the air from in front of the piston in the pipe, drawing the piston along the pipe and the carriage, which is attached to the piston, is pulled along.

Two advantages over the traditional locomotive were evident to everyone. Firstly, travel on the atmospheric railway is almost silent by comparison, secondly, the lack of clouds of smoke, except at the pumping stations, would have made a refreshing change. A third advantage was not so apparent but probably even more important for these trains could not collide despite there being no on-board driver. That the air refilled the vacuum behind each carriage reducing potential motive power to a degree where it was insufficient to move it until the previous carriage had passed the next pumping station. Practical problems beset the project which could not be overcome with the technologies of the day and Brunel abandoned the idea in 1848 after only a year.

Little remains of the route today, save for a pumping station near Torquay and the more obvious building at Starcross. The latter stands alongside the modern railway and is now home to the local yacht club. On the opposite side of the road we find the pub named the Atmospheric Railway. Here the sign-painter has produced an image which some may liken to a GWR King class locomotive or similar. Clearly, this individual never took the slightest trouble to ascertain just what the atmospheric railway was.

Back of Beyond

This establishment stands on the site of a former factory, where ginger beer was produced. It later became home to a Salvation Army barracks but neither of these produced the name which simply refers to its location on the outskirts of Reading.

Bailiff's Sergeant

This pub was dedicated to the Jurates of the Level of Romney Marsh and the Office of the Bailiff's Sergeant by the brewers, recognising the work they undertook in draining the marshes and building dams to hold back the tides of the sea.

Balancing Eel

Only those with an encyclopaedic knowledge of Lewis Carol will have any idea where this name comes from. It was the name of a pub in South Shields, the name adopted when the place was refurbished following a change in ownership in 1969 until, in 2012, the building suffered a serious collapse and had to be demolished.

This is taken from a verse in Carol's *Alice in Wonderland* and the rhyme 'You Are Old, Father William'. The seventh of the eight verses reads:

> "You are old," said the youth, "one would hardly suppose
> That your eye was as steady as ever
> Yet you balanced an eel on the end of your nose.
> What made you so awfully clever?"

The original illustrations were drawn by John Tenniel. He depicted Father William as a very rotund individual, with the eel upright on the tip of its tail and balancing on his nose. The pub sign copied the balancing act, but attached the nose to a mariner walking across the beach with his catch of fish. The name is still in use at the opposite end of England, by a fish and chip shop in St Ives, Cornwall.

Banker's Draft

The building was constructed for the York and County Bank and opened in 1904. By the end of the First World War it was a branch of the Midland Bank and remained such until 1989. The pub name refers to its former use as a bank with the second element a play on words – it alludes to the present use where draught beer is sold, while also linking to the previous use with the term bank draft.

Whilst the bank draft performs the same function as a cheque, it transfers money from one account to another without handling physical cash, the cheque does not transfer the cash amount until the cheque is paid into the recipient's account. In the case of a draft, the money is transferred to the bank's account, and thus deducted from the first account, as soon as it is raised meaning, unlike a cheque, a draft cannot bounce.

Barking Smack

A name often misunderstood, especially by those who are unaware that Barking refers to a place in Essex, and that a smack is a single-masted sailing vessel used to catch mackerel off the coast of Great Yarmouth.

Barmy Arms

If we were to rely on the sign to define this name we would never find the truth. The term 'arms' was used so often to show the sign featured elements from a coat of arms, it effectively became a synonym for 'pub'. Here the sign painter has turned this around, using 'arms' to develop a fictional shield with quarters showing various images designed to illustrate just how 'barmy' this 'arms' is. From top left and reading clockwise we find: a coiled party horn; Mad-Hatter's hat, complete with price tag of 10 shillings and six pence; a joke pair of glasses complete with false nose and moustache and a banana skin. Of course, the modern idea is of the Barmy Army, the adopted name of followers of the English cricket team.

The term 'barmy' comes from 'barm', in this context nothing to do with the bread roll of northern England but a reference to the foamy scum forming on the surface of fermenting brews. Thus 'likened to barm' or 'barmy' began as identifying someone who, as in the fermentation process, had something of little use up top!

Baron Cadogan

A pub in Caversham which recalls Caversham Park and its role as the seat of William, Viscount Caversham and Baron Cadogan of Reading, who was Commander-in-Chief of the British Army.

Bay Horse

A bay horse is a very specific description of a brown horse, be it light or dark brown, having black points – ie the mane and tail. This made for a sign all would recognise but one which rarely referred to a specific animal.

Bear and Dragon

An establishment which opened in the 1930s as simply the Bear. When the pub closed shortly after the millennium celebrations, it was three years before it reopened as the Bear and Dragon. Whilst the original name may have some connections to heraldry, the same is not true of the addition which was inspired by the new premises specialising in Thai cuisine.

Bee

At Whittlesey, in Cambridgeshire, was once found this pub, an unfortunate error for the name was originally the Letter B. This was not the only pub with this kind of name for there had also been pubs named the Letter A and the Letter C, both of which have now closed. Researchers have suggested there were once as many as 52 pubs open at one time in Whittlesey.

Bees in the Wall
At Whittlesford, in Cambridgeshire, is a delightfully different pub name which would clearly have reflected bee-keeping. That the bees were 'in the wall' is no surprise, bee-keepers would often create an artificial hibernation cavity in a wall in order to prevent their precious colony from swarming elsewhere.

Beetle and Wedge
This is a former boathouse which still has its feet in the Thames, although its slipway has not been used since 1967. However, this name has no connection to a boathouse nor the insect, for here the 'beetle' is a large mallet which drives the wedge into logs to split them into more usable diameters. Once these logs were floated downriver from the local woodland to London where greater demand produced a quicker sale and at a better price.

Bel and the Dragon
A pub name derived from two stories, both found in the Bible and the Book of Daniel. In one he refuses to believe that Bel is a Babylonian god because he eats food and thus is only human, showing he is fed by priests through a secret doorway. The second narrative tells of him slaying a dragon, for which he is cast into the lions' den where he is unharmed.

Bell on the Green
The very epitome of a village pub name for it speaks of the village green and the church, invariably the centre of the place, and also tells the potential customer exactly where to find the establishment.

THE BELL ON THE GREEN

Bell and Jorrocks

At Frittenden, in Kent, is this pub name which was once two separate premises. The former name is easy to see as showing this was land belonging to the church, while John Jorrocks is a character created by 19th century novelist Robert Surtees. Jorrocks was a Cockney grocer, whose unique personality led him into a series of adventures.

Bells of Ouseley

A pub name which corrupts the Oxfordshire place name of Ousley. Its connection to Old Windsor, where it is to be found, is through the bells, Osney Abbey having a famous set of bells, the biggest of which was Great Tom, brought here at the time of the Dissolution.

Bettle and Chisel

As with the Beetle and Wedge, this is a mallet used with a wide sharp edge to split the end product. Here in Cornwall it was used on slate in the nearby quarries.

Bishop Blaize Inn

A present-day Manchester pub named after its predecessor, which stood on this site from the 15th century until the middle of the 19th century. Bishop Blaize was chosen as he is the patron saint of woolcombers, once an important trade in this region.

Bishop's Finger

What is now better known as a brand of real ale had long been the name of a couple of pubs in the religious strongholds of Canterbury and London. The term had been in use long before that as a reference to a signpost, from there transferred to a nearby pub.

To previous generations the signpost, more commonly referred to as a fingerpost, was known as a Bishop's Finger as it pointed the way while never taking that way itself. The name hints that the churchman was the same, pointing the righteous way but perhaps not practising what he preaches.

Black Horse

A common enough pub name and one with a number of plausible origins. Doubtless the vast majority originate in heraldry, a part of the arms of a family or landholder. As a name it has also been used to refer to the 7th Dragoon Guards, who had black trim on their uniforms and did ride black horses. It has also been used for trades, notably a well-known high street bank but also the goldsmiths of Lombard Street in London.

Black Swan

Until the middle of the 18th century every mature swan in the world had white feathers, or so it was thought. It was in 1770 when Captain James Cook landed in Botany Bay that the native Australian population of black swans were discovered. This bird is now found in New Zealand, having been taken there to replace the New Zealand black swans which had been hunted to extinction by the Maoris years before.

Oddly, there were pubs in Britain named the Black Swan by the 16th century, over 250 years before the birds were known. Even earlier, in the second century AD, the Roman writer and satirist Juvenal wrote of the black swan stating it was a rare bird indeed. This was also intended to show all swans were white and a black version would be a very special find. This resulted in the black swan's use in heraldry and soon afterwards in pub names.

Bladebone

A pub named after a large bone of some unrecorded prehistoric animal was found at nearby Bucklebury Common in Berkshire.

Blind Beggar

A pub with a long history and one named after Henry, the son of Simon de Montfort. He was badly injured and left for dead at the Battle of Evesham in 1265. Found to be alive, he was recognised and nursed back to health by a baroness, with whom he later had a daughter. Returning to London he became known as the Blind Beggar of Bethnal Green, where he was often seen begging at the crossroads.

The story may well have been forgotten were it not for a revival 300 years after his death, when it became a popular tale during the Tudor era. Later the tale enjoyed a third lease of life in the 19th century as the eponymous figure in a popular ballad.

Blink Bonny

In Alnwick, Northumberland, is a pub named after a filly which hit the headlines in 1857 for both the right and the wrong reasons. As a two-year-old this blazed-faced and undersized racing horse won eight of its 11 starts. Next year it started a further 20 races, winning 14. Among its wins were the Derby by a neck and the Oaks by an impressive eight lengths. Jockey John Charlton was blamed for her defeat in the 1,000 Guineas and the St Leger. Indeed, it was claimed he had been paid to throw the race particularly as Imperieuse was the victor on both occasions.

Blinking Owl

These premises were formerly known as the Bakers Arms. Business was ticking over without realising its true potential until new ownership saw a real family effort breathe new life into the place.

One of the first decisions was to change the name, yet they had no idea of what to change the name to. Another obvious failing was the space taken up by the old barn. Now it houses an exquisite restaurant and provides accommodation, yet when the family arrived it was used solely for storing wood. At the time this was the only fuel for heating the rooms in the pub and needed to be replenished before both morning and evening sessions – this was before licensing laws were relaxed and pubs could remain open all day.

Gathering enough willing pairs of hands to carry the supply of logs, the family would head for the old barn. Yet, seemingly, every time the door opened in the evening the resident barn owl chose that moment to exit its roost. With soundless beating wings in the evening gloom, often all that could be noted was the breeze as it passed just inches over their heads. It was then the new name was blurted out as someone would inevitably exclaim – "That blinking owl!"

The tale does not end there for the Blinking Owl public house required a sign. Both daughters were keen and talented artists and the task was given to one of them. She delighted in producing the sign which still adorns the public house and is the epitome of a family business.

Blue Bell

Note how many public houses put these two words together to become the Bluebell. Even when they correctly show two words, invariably the sign depicts the popular woodland springtime flower. However, the real origin is in religion, represented by the bell and where 'blue' points specifically to Christianity.

Blue Lagoon

The Blue Lagoon shares its name with the only nature reserve near Milton Keynes. This is the site of an old brickworks, the bricks being made from clay extracted from the belt of clay extending here from Oxfordshire. This site was closed in 1970 and subsequently flooded when the Water Eaton Brook burst its banks. The blue colour of the water, which gives this place its name, is created by the colour of the clay lake bed.

Blue Lias

Near Stockton, in Warwickshire, is this unusual name taken from the rocks hereabouts which have been mined for many years and used in the production of cement. These were laid down in the Jurassic period, hence the sign features an image of a Diplodocus.

Blue Monkey

The natural harbour at Plymouth has always been associated with the sea. While stories have been told of monkeys on the roof and well-attired mascots, the true origin has to be the powder monkeys. These young boys of 12 to 14 years of age, chosen for their below-average height and speed, would scurry around below decks bringing gunpowder from the store to those loading the canons. This would leave a blue residue on their hands and led to them being known as Blue Powder Monkeys.

Blue Raddle

A Dorset pub with a name referring to a door or gate made by weaving wooden laths between stronger upright poles, or raddles, the colour can only be pertinent to this place.

Boater

A Bedfordshire pub having nothing to do with the water but the straw hat. Luton was the hub of the straw-plaiting industry from the 17th century, this was made into the hard straw hat which is so often associated with boating, hence the name of the hat being the boater and from there the pub. This town later made headwear from felt and is still associated with hatting, the nearby Luton football team are nicknamed The Hatters.

Bollin Fee

This is an old place name, one of the four which were combined in the late 19th century to produce the town of Wilmslow, Cheshire.

Boot

At Soulbury, in Buckinghamshire, the public house named the Boot sees sign painters readily link to the famed footwear of the Duke of Wellington. However, the Soulbury Boot is a legend which pre-dates the renowned soldier and politician by centuries. It was during a time when the Devil himself paid a visit to the village. Clearly, the villagers were afraid but, determined to rid themselves of this evil, gathered together to fight off this enemy. During the battle one man brought his sword down and severed the foot of the Devil. Immediately, it turned to stone and remained in the village, thereafter known as the Soulbury Boot. While many legends have some basis in fact, this narrative was almost certainly created by a former landlord of the Boot in order to entertain and attract customers.

Boot and Shoe

At Scotforth, in Lancashire, is this pub named from the story of John Schorne, a priest from the 13th century who is said to have tricked the Devil and he became trapped in his boot. Never beatified he has always been regarded as the peasants' saint.

Boot and Slipper

A reminder of the 13th century priest John Schorne, who is said to have imprisoned the Devil in a boot. He was not considered for beatification for this act, yet he has always been regarded as the peasants' saint. The same story is seen under the Devil in the Boot.

Brains Surgery

So often written 'Brain Surgery', this pub in Bath was the first on the English side to offer beer from the Brains Brewery of Wales. Clearly the 'Surgery' was something of a tongue-in-cheek addition, but used in the same context as a meeting place makes perfect sense.

Bransty Arch

A pub in Whitehaven named after the arch that allowed coal to come from Whingill Pits to be loaded on to the ships on the North Shore and shipped to Ireland. The arches were a part of the town and it was a sad day when the arches were demolished in 1927, deemed necessary as the new bus services were unable to pass beneath.

Brass Balance

The pub stands on the site of a former Birkenhead factory. The well-known name of W & T Avery were manufacturers of brass balances and other machines used for weighing. Their name can still be found on scales throughout the country.

Brass Cat

As with the Mad Cat this is a local name for an image which is officially a golden lion, the original name of the Halifax premises. Here the local name has been adopted officially.

Brawn Queen

At Yoxford, in Suffolk, is a pub with a story to tell. The first Sunday after Easter each year is when the village holds a brawn-eating competition, although for reasons unknown it is known locally as 'pork cheese' instead of brawn. This does not stop the Brawn Queen being known as such, the elected lady's task is but to ceremoniously cut the brawn or cheese.

British Volunteer

Just one of a number of this name is found at Weybridge, in Surrey. Different signs depict the name from different eras, some as recently as the 12th century and the Home Guard, others the First World War and the Volunteer Training Corps. Most show the soldier volunteering to fight for his country against the threat of invasion by Napoleonic France.

Brun Lea

This pub uses the original Saxon name of the place where brun lea refers to 'the brown meadow' and is today the town of Burnley.

Bucket of Blood

It is no coincidence to find that many early pubs were built adjacent to a well. Today, real ale drinkers seek out micro-breweries for their distinctive tipples, yet once this was the norm for pubs invariably brewed their own ales. No matter how good the yeast, barley, hops, etc., without a reliable and clean supply of water there would be nothing to quench the thirsts of the customers. Thus the well has been used to name a number of pubs, patrons recognising the message of a good source of clean water.

One well name is found in the shape of the Jack and Jill at Coulsdon, Surrey. Here the pub stands on a hill and, during extensive rebuilding work in the 1950s, when a well was discovered at the back of the premises the nursery rhyme characters almost suggested themselves. In contrast, the local at Phillack, Cornwall, is certainly not as suitable for the very young nor indeed a good advertisement for the well.

A landlord during the late 18th century ventured out to the well as he had done countless times before. Dropping his bucket down the well he heard the expected splash and wound the now much heavier bucket back to the top. It was then he got the shock of his life. While the bucket should have contained refreshing cool fresh water, what he saw was red blood both filling and spilling down the side of the container.

Later examination revealed a badly mutilated corpse had been thrown down the well. It seems the crime was never solved, nor the victim identified, yet the tale was told and retold down the years until what was then the New Inn was renamed in the 1980s to reflect the local name of the establishment. Today the horror of the discovery is graphically retold in sign outside the Bucket of Blood.

Bull and Spectacles

A Staffordshire establishment whose name is said to be derived from the exploits of a prize-winning specimen. The bull nearly lost its life after eating poisonous berries and a local is reputed to have suggested spectacles might prevent a second occurrence.

Bull i' th' Thorn

The definition of this name has been heavily influenced by a carving inside the establishment showing such an animal entangled in a thorn bush. Undoubtedly, this would explain the name, providing the name came after, or was contemporary with, the carving of wood taken from an oak tree. There is more than a little evidence to suggest the name already existed before the tree was felled, although it would take tree ring dating to prove so conclusively.

It must be said the whole idea of a bull being entangled in a thorn bush leading to any name would be unusual. Place names of any description rely on the name being relevant, and any animal trapped would surely only be a matter of days at most, certainly not enough to produce a name. Yet is there an alternative explanation? The answer is affirmative and produces a much more plausible explanation.

It is suggested this was not the original name, although the current name has been recorded since the 15th century, and it was formerly known as simply the Bull. After a particularly stormy winter someone noticed the pub sign had disappeared. An extensive search revealed nothing and after time the episode was almost forgotten. Almost, that is, until the winter chills took the leaves from the trees and, there in the midst of a nearby thorn bush, was the now rather weather-beaten sign of the Bull.

In truth, both stories are equally suspect, the second explanation only favoured as the name would have been based on events over a number of months, not a few days.

Bull Inn

As with the Black Horse this is a name that has several possible origins and it is difficult to know which is the real source. Most are undoubtedly heraldic, the strong image of the bull chosen by any number of families and also trades such as the Butchers Company. It could also be a religious reference, in particular Catholicism and the papal bull.

Bunch of Carrots

At Hampton Bishop, in Herefordshire, is a pub named after the rock formation alongside the waters of the River Wye and said to resemble such, although clearly named by someone with a very vivid imagination.

Bun Penny

At Herne, in Kent, is the Queen Victoria, another of the many examples that also makes our second-longest reigning monarch (after our current Queen, Elizabeth II) the woman with the most pubs named after her. This is not the only pub in Herne to be named after the queen, although there would probably be some confusion unless you could see the sign outside the Bun Penny. This refers to the image of the queen on the penny black, the first stamp issued anywhere in the world, where she is wearing her hair in a bun.

Busby Stoop

Thomas Busby was a coiner and renowned drunkard who was hanged at the crossroads on the stoop or post alongside the inn which was later to bear his name and his fate.

Busby managed to win the heart and hand of the local beauty, Elizabeth Auty, very much against the wishes of her father, Daniel Auty. Even their marriage did not deter her father from trying to persuade her to return to the family home. One evening in 1702, Busby came home to find his father-in-law seated in his favourite chair and vowing to take his daughter home. Having failed again, Auty returned to his home and died later that night, strangled in his own bed by Busby. At his subsequent execution, the murderer was far from repentant, indeed he seemed more concerned with his chair and cursed any who should ever dare sit in it.

It is claimed Busby's ghost still roams the site of his execution, while the infamous chair still exists and is said to have been behind the deaths of no less than 63 individuals. Among those who died shortly after taking their ease here were Carlo Pagnani, who had his own furniture repair business, and two RAF airmen. Today the chair hangs in Thirsk Museum. Yes, hangs. It is suspended from the ceiling to prevent anyone from ever taking a seat here again.

Byards Leap

A Sheffield public house that commemorates a Lincolnshire place name and story. It was here a witch known as Old Meg drove the villagers to distraction with her curses and spells. As crops continued to wither they cried out for someone to aid them in their plight.

An old soldier answered their calls and promised to kill the witch by plunging his sword straight through her heart. Before setting out for Old Meg's haunt at High Dike, he needed a horse and so made his way to the village pond. Throwing a stone into the water he selected the steed with the quickest reaction. This was Blind Byard, a horse that had been blind for as long as anyone had known.

On reaching Old Meg's cave he demanded she come out to face him, but she refused saying she was eating. However, this was a ruse to distract him and she crept out and leapt upon the horse's back, sinking her long nails into its flesh. Understandably, the horse fled in terror, witnesses saying the beast cleared 60 feet in a single leap. It took the soldier until they reached the pond to regain control of his mount, where Old Meg caught up with them only to end her life as the soldier turned and killed her with a single thrust. The place where the horse landed is marked by four posts, with a horseshoe nailed to each, around a commemorative stone.

Calcaria

A public house named after the Roman town in the province of Britannia. Today the place is known as Tadcaster.

Cannard's Grave

Not just a pub name but also a hamlet. It is said both remember Giles Cannard, a 17th century landlord of the local inn – which clearly had another name then, one unfortunately unknown – whose meagre earnings from the inn tempted him to turn to crime.

He is by no means the only landlord who used what he had overheard from his guests to line his coffers. Passing on details of destination, route, cargo and valuables to his associates he received a cut. Cannard is also suspected of smuggling and forgery. He was certainly gibbetted here and buried at the crossroads.

Captain Fryatt

At Harwich, in Essex, we find a pub named after a man who hit the headlines in 1916. A merchant seaman who could not have envisaged the month in store for him when in command of SS *Wrexham* in March 1915. His vessel was attacked by a German U-Boat but escaped to Rotterdam. Later that month, he commanded SS *Colchester* when it was unsuccessfully attacked, then he was captain of SS *Brussels* when a third attack ensued. Seeing he was about to be torpedoed Fryatt attempted to ram the submarine, which only escaped by crash diving. Fryatt was arrested in June the next year and charged with sinking a submarine that was still in full working order. He faced a court-martial, despite being a civilian, and died in front of a firing squad on 27 July 1916. This action was almost universally condemned and, after the war, his body was exhumed from the 'Belgian traitor cemetery' outside Bruges and returned to Britain where he was given a funeral at St Paul's Cathedral when he was also awarded the Belgian Order of Leopold and Belgian Maritime War Cross.

Captain Mannering

A name inspired by the leader of the Home Guard in the much-loved BBC sitcom *Dad's Army* and the nearby army camp. Apparently, not everyone watched the broadcasts (or the many repeats), including the sign painter who was seemingly unaware the character's name was pronounced 'Mannering' but should be spelled 'Mainwaring'. In recent years the name has been changed to the Garrison Arms.

Carlbury Arms

One of many pubs simply named to show their location. However, it seems unlikely the owners will have been aware they were referring to a place name meaning 'the fortified place of the peasants'.

Carpenters Arms

While modern signs tend to show heraldic images and modern tools, early signs simply used the basic tools of the carpenter and, in particular, the three compasses used by the Carpenters' Company.

Case is Altered

A pub named from a phrase that came to mean what, today, would be described as 'moving the goalposts'. The exact circumstances of each name is probably different, indeed the real reason is often impossible to see through a haze of folklore and legend.

WESTERHAM BREWERY

THE
CARPENTERS ARMS

Cat and Bagpipes

A North Yorkshire setting for an establishment where both elements of the name are references to Scotland. While the latter is self-explanatory as an instrument which is either loved or loathed, the former is a pointer to those who may have been playing the bagpipes. The caterans were bands of robbers who were a constant threat to the border lands.

Cat and Cabbage

A public house named after the badge of the now-disbanded regiment whose museum can be found in Rotherham. Created by the amalgamation of the 65th and 84th foot regiments, the York and Lancaster Regiment were known locally as the Cat and Cabbage. This is a reference to the regimental badge, where the two images are actually those of a tiger and a rose.

Cat and Cracker

A Kent pub named for an oil extraction plant in the Thames estuary. Here the £30 million plant produced a million tons of crude oil annually which was processed using a refining method to increase the proportion of usable and more valuable products in, what was known as, catalytic cracking and led to the name of the public house.

Cat and Custard Pot

A pub in Folkestone, Kent, which was, for much of its life, known as the Red Lion. As with several odd pub names this has, at least in part, come from the rather unkind local reference to the image on the sign.

During a storm, many years ago, the sign hanging outside the Red Lion was blown from where it hung and ended up in a nearby tree. Beyond repair the landlord called up the talents of a local artist for a replacement. All artists are going to bring their own style into their work, thus it was never expected the old image would be seen in the new and yet people are always reluctant to see change. Hence when the fierce, yellow, blood red-eyed cat was unveiled the pub soon became known as simply 'The Cat'. Sadly, the image vanished many years ago.

When it comes to the addition it is clear the pub was known as the Cat and Mustard Pot when it was a meeting place for the East Kent Foxhounds. This is confirmed by several newspapers from around the end of the 18th and beginning of the 19th century. Just what this addition means is unknown. Yet today this place is known as the Cat and Custard Pot. Again, both when and why this change took place is unknown, although it seems safe to say this change was deliberate and thus possibly to satisfy landlords' and breweries' desire to see alliteration in pub names.

Cat and Fiddle

A pub named the Cat and Fiddle is often said to be derived from the name of Catherine la Fidele, a French woman and wife of Peter the Great of Russia (or Catherine of Aragon, depending upon the story). However, there is irrefutable evidence this name pre-dates both these women by several centuries, indeed the figure of the fiddling cat – as seen in the nursery rhyme – has been a part of the folklore of many countries since the musical instrument was first played. While the violin, in its modern form, has existed since the 16th century, the basic design has been around for at least 700 years longer.

Caxton Gibbett

Recorded here since at least the 1670s, it still overlooks the village. Where those who had been executed were displayed as a warning to others, the offender would remain here until, quite literally, the body fell apart through decomposition. The best known occupant of this gibbet was he who murdered a local man by the name of Partridge. Originally he made good his escape, but made the mistake of returning to the scene of his crime only to boast he had never been apprehended. This proved his undoing and, it is said, he was ordered to by gibbetted alive. If one version is to be believed a local baker soon joined him when he offered bread to the starving man as he hung there. This horrific form of punishment is always referred to as 'English Law', yet there is no record of this ever being practiced anywhere in England.

Cerdic
A legend from Chard in Somerset says the town was founded by one Cerdic the Saxon.

Charlaw Inn
A name taken from the local map and meaning 'the tumulus in rough ground'.

The
CHEQUERS INN

14th Century Inn

B&B

Charlton Cat

Originally this pub in Charlton St Peter was the Red Lion, later to become the Poore's Arms after the family who were lords of the neighbouring manor of Rushall during the 18th century. However, this did not prevent them from still knowing the place as the Charlton Cat, a combination of place name and a rather unkind reference to an imperfect representation of the heraldic lion.

Chequers

One of the oldest of names, certainly used by the Romans. Originally, it showed a board game could be played within but later came to be used to represent a moneylender, one such sign being found among the ruins of Herculaneum buried by Vesuvius in AD 79. Its fiscal associations are still seen in 21st century Britain, where the man holding the nation's purse strings is the Chancellor of the Exchequer.

Cherry Pickers

A delightful story lies behind the name of this Kent pub. As usual, the sign painter has been overly imaginative and not researched the origins. Here the image is shows two magpies collecting the fruit from the tree. Opting for this species of bird seems an arbitrary choice, although we should be thankful the name is not shown as the mobile platform! The name was suggested by the 11th Hussars, based at Shorncliffe, they being nicknamed the Cherry Pickers. Best remembered for their bravery in the Charge of the Light Brigade at Balaclava, they earned this nickname during another war, yet again with the French, and being the victims of a surprise attack by French cavalry – the Hussars being completely unprepared as weapons were a hindrance when picking cherries.

Cherry Tree

Another cherry name and of much simpler origin. Here the image of the tree is not used so much as a marker, although there may well have been cherry trees nearby, this is to give an instantly recognisable image of the tree in full blossom. Of course, the blossom is only visible for a couple of weeks and thus cannot be said to be a marker in the form of the actual tree, but lasts all year long on the sign.

Claude du Vall

At Camberwell, in Surrey, is a name that can be traced back to the 17th and 18th centuries, when highwaymen were the scourge of coachmen and their passengers. Camberley had two individuals whose reputation for flair and panache is, undoubtedly, a romantic notion with little or no basis in fact. Born in Normandy to once titled parents, Claude was sent to Paris at the age of 14 where he entered domestic service. This led to him find employment as a stable boy and, at the Restoration of the Monarchy, became a footman at the household of the Duke of Richmond. It is said he never once used violence to rob his victims, was known for his stylish clothes, and once agreed to restrict himself to only a portion of the money on one gentleman if his wife joined him in a dance at the roadside. Once there was a Golden Farmer pub here, too. This took the nickname of another highwayman, William Davis.

Clive and Coffyn

At Market Drayton, this name recalls the town's most famous resident, Robert Clive, who was reputed to have brought back the recipe for the small pie to which the second half of the name refers.

Clog and Billycock

Formerly known as the Bay Horse but never known as such by the Lancastrian locals. Its nickname came from licensee Alfred Pomfret who wore clogs and a billycock. The footwear was made by his brother, the billycock a style of bowler hat.

Coal Orchard

This Taunton public house was named because the nearby wharf on the River Tone had been an orchard until developed to allow the landing of coal from Wales.

Cobb Arms

This is not a family, for those who know Lyme Regis will be aware this is the name given to the harbour wall, which protects and forms the safe haven which is the harbour. Even those who have never been to the port may have unknowingly seen or read about the Cobb. An important place since the 13th century, this harbour wall has been damaged and rebuilt several times, Lyme Regis being an important port and larger than Liverpool up to the end of the 18th century, when the ships literally outgrew the place. The Cobb is an important part of Jane Austen's novel *Persuasion* and is one of the most memorable parts of the film *The French Lieutenant's Woman*, while Sir Richard Spencer RN developed the basic technology behind lifeboats here from 1824.

Cock and Pye

If not advertising the drink then promote a meal. The Cock and Pye probably points to a medieval dish of peacock pie, eating such indicated a wealthy individual. However, we cannot rule out an Elizabethan oath, where 'cock' pointed to God and 'pie' the ordinal of the Catholic Church.

Colley Rowe Inn

A pub taking the name of the road, itself reminding us this was where colliers once lived. However, note the medieval collier did not dig coal from underground seams, they smouldered stacks of wood covered in turf until the impurities were removed, leaving pure carbon which was then used just as coal was later.

Colliery

An inevitable pub name, one which grew up alongside the many coal fields of the land.

Colombia Press

In 1820 John Peacock opened his printing press in Watford, not far from this pub. The press, which produced the first edition of the *Watford Observer*, was imported from Colombia.

Colpitts Hotel

A public house named after the man who opened it, one George Colpitts. Its distinctive appearance on the hairpin bend between Allergate and Alexander Crescent makes it a well-known landmark, known as Colpitts Corner, on one of Durham's oldest streets and inhabited for more than eight centuries.

The Colpitts family certainly merit being remembered in the pub name, for not only did George run his eponymous pub but his brothers John and Thomas were then landlords of the Puncheon (later the Criterion) and Wheatsheaf respectively.

Copper Horse

A pub name coming from, of all things, a statue. Nearby is a copper statue of George III on horseback.

Cotton Bale

Hyde in Lancashire was, during the 19th century, as important a centre for cotton as almost anywhere in the Cheshire and Lancashire area.

Craven Heifer

At Clitheroe, in Lancashire, is a public house named after one of the most famous animals ever to graze the pastures of England. Bred by the Rev W. Carr, in 1807, on the Duke of Devonshire's estate. As it grew it was soon realised this was a magnificent beast, eventually reaching a length of 11 feet 4 inches (3.45 metres) without the tail and tipping the scales at 312 stones 8 pounds (1,985 kilograms). Sold to a Mr John Watkinson for £200 he was taken on a tour of England, the 73-day journey led by a Mr Pickop and a Mr Kitchen ending at Smithfield. The latter gentleman's surname was to prove prophetic for the beast was put up as the stake in a cockfight. The backed bird was defeated and the Craven Heifer ended up on the butcher's slab although not yet five-years-old.

Crooked House

A pub near Himley, in the Black Country, where subsidence has resulted in a building that lives up to its name. Scheduled for demolition in the 1940s, it was saved when the brewery rescued it with a system of buttresses and girders. Despite the building being secured it is still quite a strange experience to discover an object will apparently roll uphill along a table or window sill. Of course the laws of physics still apply here and this is purely an optical illusion created by the rebuild to correct one end of the premises being four feet lower than the other.

Crown and Two Chairmen

It is said this place was named after Queen Anne came to sit for the parts of her portrait that could not be done in her absence. Artist

Sir James Thornhill is held to have had the studio opposite the pub. Known as the Crown until two years after the artist's death in 1734, the addition is said to refer to the two who brought Her Majesty here in a sedan chair and would partake of the refreshment on offer here while the queen was posing.

Cuckoo's Nest

As we learn from a very young age, the cuckoo makes no nest but lays its eggs in the nest of other birds and allows them to rear its young. Thus the name is telling us this is a very special place, something so rare as to be unique, which is not quite true for there are other pubs of this name elsewhere in the country.

Cunning Man

Here the sign depicts said man of cunning leaning over into a stream. The image is that of a man tickling trout, a process which involves reaching into the trout's hiding place and tickling its belly. The fish reacts by going into an almost trance-like state, slipping back into the hands and is caught when the tickler can catch the fish by the gills. This method is illegal in Britain, principally as it was employed by poachers who, if caught, had no evidence such as rods and nets on their person.

Dairy Maid

An old coaching inn that took its name from the stagecoach which ran through Aylesbury en route from London and Buckingham. On 20 June 1815 it brought news of the victory over Napoleon at Waterloo, just two days after the battle had ended, an event recorded inside the pub.

Dandy Lion

To hear the name of this pub in Bradford on Avon, in Wiltshire, would immediately put one in mind of the weed, the bane of gardeners everywhere. However, the sign shows the king of beasts dressed in the most elegant of attire, a truly Dandy Lion.

Daniel Lambert

This remembers the man born in Leicester in March 1770, his link to Stamford being through his uncle, gamekeeper to the Earl of Stamford, and his great-uncle, huntsman to the Earl of Stamford, while it was the town where he died. A period as an apprentice in Birmingham's jewellery quarter ended with the Birmingham Riots of 1791 and he returned to his native Leicester to take over from his father as keeper of the bridewell, a house of correction run by local magistrates. Looking after five rooms, three for male and two for female prisoners, earned them the princely sum of £21 a year, the remainder of their income came through the labour exacted from their charges. His childhood saw him excel as a swimmer, later he excelled at field and gun sports, and was considered an excellent horseman despite tipping the scales at 32 stones by 1793. By 1804 his weight had reached 49 stones and he had a special carriage to convey him to London, where he was to allow himself to be observed as 'a curiosity' and within a couple of years was on tour in the Midlands. Despite it being claimed he ate only heartily, never to excess, by the time he died in Stamford on 21 June 1809 this man, just an inch under 6 feet in height, weighed 52 stones and 11 pounds.

Delabole

The public house is named after the village which, in turn, is named after the Delabole Quarry. The place name comes from the Cornish *poll* meaning 'pit' and the local stream name Delyow.

Devil in the Boot

At Winslow, in Buckinghamshire, this pub is named from the story of John Schorne, a 13th century priest said to have tricked the Devil resulting in him becoming trapped in Schorne's boot. At nearby North Marston, Schorne Lane is a reminder of the Schorne Well, also known as Holy Well, both derived from the former rector of the parish, Sir St John Schorne. His discovery of the well during a particularly severe drought made him famous. Later claims suggested the waters were a cure for gout and toothache. Recently the well, a place of pilgrimage following Schorne's death, was renovated. This late 13th century figure is often referred to as a saint although, of course, this was just his name, and while never beatified he has always been hailed as the peasants' saint. The Boot and Shoe at Scotforth in Lancashire and the Eels Foot in Eastbridge, Suffolk are from the same story.

Devil's Stone Inn

The unusual name becomes a little more obvious when visiting for there is a one ton lump of rock in Shebbear, Devon, which is very difficult to miss. This boulder is a glacial erratic, not of local stone but carried and dropped here by a glacier as it melted at the end of the last ice age. Folklore maintains it was dropped here by Satan as he passed by, eventually dying from the cold in nearby Northlew. Tradition also maintains that the stone be turned every year. Hence on 5 November each year, while the youngsters are enjoying fireworks, a select few head off to the stone and turn it over to ward off evil. Within memory only twice has the stone been left, the last time during the Second World War when such was seen as a frivolous waste of time and energy. Yet when news from the war effort was nothing but doom and gloom for several days, the light of day revealed the stone had been turned by persons unknown.

Dick Turpin

Premises named to mark the famous highwayman's ride from London to York on his horse, Black Bess. Turpin was hanged outside York and, we are told, buried, with his horse, in a grave at Fishergate, York. Many doubt whether Turpin is actually here, and Black Bess most certainly is not for his famous horse and he had parted company some years earlier. It will come as no surprise to find this story is entirely fictitious, 200 miles in a single day for any horse (other than the winged horse Pegasus from Greek mythology) is quite impossible. Yet the story had been told many times before Turpin was even born. Daniel Defoe, writing about his tour of Britain in 1727, told of William Nevison riding from London to York 50 years earlier to establish an alibi and remove himself from suspicion of a crime he certainly committed. This became established in folklore, as it probably had been even before Defoe put pen to paper, and was never attributed to Turpin until 1867 when William Harrison Ainsworth wrote a serialised and fictitious account in the popular Victorian publications known as penny dreadfuls.

Dinton Hermit

A pub name with a story to tell. In 1596 one John Brigg was born here, an educated man he became a trusted adviser of Oliver Cromwell. He achieved unwanted fame as one of the judges who passed sentence on Charles I which, following the execution of the king, affected his mental health. Other sources suggest he was executioner. Brigg returned to the area of his birth, becoming a recluse and relying on handouts of bread and ale from friends. One of the friends was Simon Mayne, another regicide, who lived at Dinton and died in imprisonment in 1661, whereupon his body was returned to Dinton. In truth, the story of John Brigg being a hermit and forced to live off handouts, makes more sense if he was the executioner and those responsible would naturally have taken care of the man who dealt the fatal blow.

Doctor Syntax

A pub named after a thoroughbred who had a record, in the early 19th century, as a stayer. The horse dominated distance events in the north of England throughout his career. That he never won any of the flat race classics is nothing to do with ability, this was down to horses being walked to courses before rail travel became commonplace.

The horse was named from a character created by writer William Combe, who penned a series of comic verse entitled 'The Three Tours of Dr Syntax'. These were illustrated by Thomas Rowlandson, indeed it was the illustrations which led to the popularity of the series and the naming of the horse.

Dog and Doublet

The present building at Sandon, in Staffordshire, only dates from the early 12th century, taking its name from its predecessor on this site named following the landlord's murder by robbers. His faithful dog removed his master's blood-stained doublet and, after bringing it to the inn, led searchers to the body. The original sign depicted the dog wearing a doublet. In the heyday of the coaching era the inn was an important and well-known stopping place.

Dog and Duck

Nearly always found near the site of the village pond, the Dog and Duck recalls a sport much favoured by Charles II. Ducks had their wings pinned to prevent them from flying and were released on to the pond. When spaniels were released to catch the ducks their only means of escape was by diving.

Donkey and Buskins

Here we find a pub name inspired by a local man. Buskins are leather leggings and one considerate farmer, intending to ride his donkey back over the moor in darkness that night, decided to put them on his donkey to protect the animal's legs from the thorns which would never be seen in the dark.

Drabbet Smock

When Gurteen & Sons built their factory in 1856, it fuelled an instant expansion in the size of Haverhill which saw its population double almost overnight. The chance of work brought many to the textile factory and its 32 steam powered looms. Much of the cloth went to make the smocks worn by agricultural workers which also gave a name to the Drabbet Smock.

Dragon

Our first thought in trying to define this name is that of the mythical beast slain by England's patron saint, St George. However, it would be unique in referring the event through the bad guy and, hence, we should probably look elsewhere. Examining the sign shows this is a green dragon, rather relevant as this image points to the dukes of Pembroke, among the great landholders of England. To assume the Dragon has lost its colour makes more sense than a reverse reference to a patriotic establishment.

Drunken Duck

At this pub in Hawkshead, Lancashire, the lady of the inn discovered a number of their domestic waterfowl lying flat out in the yard at the back of the establishment. Closer inspection revealed they were not dead but dead drunk, having eaten grain which was soaked in ale seeping from a leaky barrel in the yard.

Duke of Kent

A pub named after the dukedom created on 23 April 1799 to King George III's fourth son, Prince Edward Augustus. The duke did little to rewrite the pages of history, not even having a son to inherit the title. He did, however, have one child – a daughter, Princess Alexandrina Victoria, who became Queen Victoria.

Duke of Northumberland

A pub named for the nobles residing at nearby Alnwick Castle. Probably the most infamous was the first creation, John Dudley, 1st Earl of Warwick. In 1553 it was he who pushed the claim of his daughter-in-law to the throne of England. Sadly, history records what happened to Lady Jane Grey, the nine day queen – less well known is how Dudley suffered the same fate.

Duke of York

Any child will tell you the rhyme, where he marched his 10,000 men up and down hills. However, this rhyme is highly inaccurate, for the Grand Old Duke of York in question was Frederick Augustus, second son of George III. He was a military leader and, undoubtedly, grand but not old, he was just 31 when he led his men, so certainly not old. He commanded 30,000 men, three times that in the rhyme, and they never had to negotiate inclines for the campaign was in Flanders, one of the flattest regions of Europe.

Dukes Head

A common enough name and one which normally features the head and shoulders of the Duke of Wellington or Duke of York. However, in Hamstreet, in Kent, the Dukes Head shows an image of Prince Adolphus, Duke of Cambridge from 1801 until his death in 1850. He was given the title as the tenth child, seventh son, of George III and Queen Charlotte. Two of his brothers ascended to the throne as William IV and George IV, while his great-great-granddaughter was crowned at Westminster Abbey in June 1953 and became the second-longest serving monarch in British history, after our current Queen, Elizabeth II.

Dumb Bell

Outside this pub in Maidenhead hangs the image of a young woman hanging from the clapper of a bell and is not quite as politically incorrect as it seems. Here, the message it carries refers to the dumbing of the bell, for if she manages to prevent the bell from ringing it will not toll for the execution of her love – or so she believes.

Eagle and Child

A name found in several places around the country, a device taken from the coat of arms of the Stanley family, earls of Derby. It is said the image was adopted after their ancestor, Sir Thomas Latham, had an illegitimate son in the 14th century. Wanting to make the child his heir he had it placed under a tree, one where an eagle had its nest, and where it was found by himself and his wife as they wandered this estate and adopted as their own. Whether Sir Thomas had a change of heart in later years is unknown but we do know the boy did not inherit. That went to Isobel, his daughter, who married Sir John Stanley thus uniting the estate, the name and the image of the eagle and child.

Eclipse

When a new pub was built the name would often be as simplistic as the New Inn, an indication as to which was the most recently built and likely the more comfortable and hospitable. One of the most common names was the Sun Inn, when a new pub was built it would often be named thus to literally 'eclipse' the competition.

Edmund Tylney

A Leatherhead pub named after the local man who was Master of Revels to both Elizabeth I and James I.

Edward Rayne

A station and rural development named after the landowner, Edward Rayne.

Edwin Waugh

At Heywood is this pub named after a poet sometimes describes as the 'Burns of Lancashire', as he was known, a 19th century dialect poet.

Elephant and Castle

A name which continues to be explained as a corruption of the Infanta de Castile. Doubtless this creative etymology will continue despite this being far from the true origin. As with many pub names, this is heraldic, representing a trade. Here we see the crest of the Cutler's Company, the link to elephants through the use of ivory as handles, while the 'castle' is always depicted on the back of the animal and is actually a howdah.

Ell's Foot

At Ormesby, in Norfolk, is a public house with a name corrupted from 'Devil's Foot' or 'Devil's Boot'. This is a reminder of the tale of the parish priest who managed to trap and tie the Devil in his boot, ridding the parish of evil by tossing the lot into the sea.

Engine

At Ashwell, in Hertfordshire, is a pub name which has lost its second element for this was originally the Engine and Drum. Here the 'drum' was part of the cylindrical threshing machine powered by the steam engine, with the whole assembly mounted on top of a horse-drawn wagon. Such a sight must have made a terrific impression on the villagers.

Enigma

At Borehamwood, in Hertfordshire, we find a reminder of the enigma machine, the German coding machine that enabled them to send covert messages over long distances with little risk of them being understood, even if they were intercepted. Famously, British workers managed to break the code and, unknown to the Nazis, were aware of their plans. This was a major factor in bringing the war to a quick conclusion and the reason for the naming of the Enigma public house.

Eric Bartholomew

Fittingly, this pub is in Morecambe as this was the name of Eric Morecambe, the taller and funnier half of the Morecambe and Wise partnership. He chose the name during a train journey as the pair were travelling to their next booking.

Ernehale

This is the Old English or Saxon name for Arnold in Nottinghamshire where the modern pub is found today. The name means 'eagle's nest'.

Eva Hart

At Chadwell Heath, in Essex, we find a pub remembering a lady who died in 1996 at the age of 91. She had greater cause than most to be grateful for her long life, it had nearly ended 84 years earlier when, at the age of seven, she was among those rescued from the *RMS Titanic* before it sank.

Fiddle i' th' Bag

The sign shows an image of a fiddle partially inside a velvet bag. This is said to recall a wandering fiddler who carried his instrument in such a bag and who was well known in the Warrington area. However this story is only known in connection with the public house which strongly suggests it was told after the pub was named. The real origin is the bag containing corn seed which helped the farmer in sowing.

Finnygook

A Cornish pub where the sign depicts a skeleton wearing a hat and carrying a sword in one hand and a lamp in the other along the coastline under a full moon. This is a fair representation, as indeed is the name. In Cornwall the 'gook' is the ghost of a man named Finny. He was a real person, a smuggler, who was killed when trying to evade capture by the customs officers.

Five Alls

There are a number of pubs called the Five Alls, a name coming from the 17th century and, while there are differences between one pub and the next, shows the public house is open to all who are working together for the common good, both in and out of the pub. Most often, we see a sign where the king states, "I rule for all," the parson maintains, "I pray for all," the soldier, "I fight for all" and the labourer, "I work for all."

Five Bells

Whilst a reference to a 'bell' is invariably a reference to the church, here it may be quite different. As any sailor will know 'Five Bells' is 2:30pm on board a vessel, the end of the afternoon watch beginning at noon and indicating half an hour for every ring of the bell. Today the significance of 2:30pm is lost with day-long opening hours, yet once 2:30pm signaled the end of the lunchtime session at the public house and this could easily be the reason it was chosen.

Five Miles from Anywhere No Hurry Inn

Originally this pub in Upware, Cambridgeshire, was opened in 1760 to serve river traffic and known as the Black Swan until, in 1805, changed its name to the Lord Nelson to commemorate the Battle of Trafalgar fought in October of that year. However, by the middle of the 19th century it had become known as the Five Miles from Anywhere: No Hurry – a name coined, depending upon which source is trusted, either by a man called Fielder who was the self-proclaimed King of Upware and a boat-builder, who spent his spare time drinking excessively, or the Upware Republic, a group of Cambridge undergraduates who came here for 'hunting, shooting and fishing'. The difference between the modern name and the earlier, unofficial, name started in the 1950s when the thatched building was largely destroyed by fire and had to be demolished. The present building dates from the 1980s when the end was changed to 'No Hurry Inn', a pun aimed at the leisure boaters on the River Cam.

Five Quarter
A Peterlee pub named after one of the coal seams at the Horden Colliery, then the biggest pit in the land.

Flying Bedstead
During the early 1960s the earliest designs for the Harrier Jump Jet was tested near this pub in Hucknall, Nottinghamshire. The Harrier was the first VTOL (Vertical Take-Off and Landing) aeroplane, although the first working experimental designs bore no resemblance to any aircraft but, as the pub sign showed, looked just like its nickname of the flying bedstead.

Ford Madox Brown
A Manchester pub named after the artist who has two of his most famous works hanging in the nearby Manchester City Art Gallery.

Four Alls
The Four Alls public house is a name most often found in the West Country. Here we find a sign with four individuals: the king rules for all; the priest prays for all; the soldier fights for all; and the labourer works for all. There is also a version with five characters, with both carrying the message that no matter how important or powerful the individual none of the others could exist without the worker supporting the whole structure.

Four Candles
Anyone of a certain age will associate this phrase with the Two Ronnies, and this sketch is exactly where the name comes from. This pub is not far from the City of Oxford High School for Boys, one former pupil being Ronnie Barker who wrote the sketch where he walks into a hardware store and apparently askes for 'four candles', but when these are placed before him he reiterates he actually asked for 'fork handles' and the same theme continues throughout the sketch.

Four Counties

The village of No Man's Heath is officially in Staffordshire. Its name informs us it has been disputed territory for at least as long as it has been known as such. The local here was the Four Counties, said to be the point where Staffordshire, Warwickshire, Leicestershire and Derbyshire met. This is not in any way correct, and never has been, but did not stop the stories proliferating. This building will have had more than one room – a bar, a lounge, a smoke room, an outdoor area, perhaps even a gentleman's only room at one stage – and it is said those enjoying a drink in the bar who were being sought by the law in one county had only to slip through to the lounge to evade capture as they had no powers in the adjoining county. Even if the building had had a wall in every county the boundaries were no barrier to the law.

Fox and Goose

When it comes to pub names, the Fox and Goose is invariably depicted as the predator with its prey and yet the true origin could not be more different. Very early examples were actually a political comment, where the fox represented the church and the goose was the land being snapped up the rich church with no regard to the people who relied on the land just to survive. Later the Fox and Goose showed a game was played within, a form of Nine Men's Morris, a board game of strategy developed by the Roman Empire.

Friar Penketh

Stands on the Warrington site of a 13th century Augustinian friary. One of their number, that of Friar Penketh, is known as he is mentioned in Shakespeare's *Richard III*.

Froize

A Suffolk pub which has traditionally been said to have come from the name of savoury pancake, one served with bacon, and derived from a French recipe. Yet the simple and most obvious origin does not seem to satisfy the villagers of Chillesford, who prefer the idea of the local pronunciation of 'friars'. In truth, these premises are located on Friar's Walk and close to Butley Priory, yet this may easily be mere coincidence and the French pancake should not be dismissed.

However, there is one factor which should be taken into consideration and that is the age of the place as an inn. It was first licensed less than 50 years ago and first built as two adjoining gamekeeper's cottages. Today, it is one of the leading licensed restaurants in the county, rather than the traditional local of the 1970s.

Neither of the explanations seem overly plausible, while the age of the place would tend to suggest a created name. Sadly nobody bothered to record why this name was chosen and it will remain a mystery – albeit a unique name.

Frozen Mop

The locals of Mobberley, in Cheshire, agree on one thing when it comes to this name, it must have been named when a wet mop froze in cold weather. As to how this came about is rather different, there being almost as many stories as there are residents!

One of the oldest speaks of how a lady of the house would leave a mop outside the door to let her lover know when the coast was clear. Obviously, such a story would be popular but does not seem to be very practical for surely her husband would have noticed how often his wife brought the mop indoors whenever he appeared. Another popular explanation refers to the local rugby team on a training run seeing the mop frozen into the mop bucket as a permanent fixture outside the pub. Again this hardly seems likely, for even in the worst of winters a thaw will have soon ruined the name. The real reason will probably never be known but it does seem more likely to have been a single incident.

Full House

Not much thought required to see a former cinema later used as a bingo hall suggesting this name. Incidentally, this building in Hemel Hempstead had its foundation stone laid by Lauren Bacall.

Gaffers Row

Crewe was once one of the great railway centres in the country. So many people earned their living from the railways terraced housing was built for some of the workforce including, near this pub, a number of properties for the gaffers – foremen or team leaders. The road named Gaffers Row can still be found a stone's throw from the pub.

Gary Cooper

A Dunstable public house named after the Oscar-winning Hollywood actor. Whilst he was born in the United States, his parents were English and chose to send both their sons to Dunstable Grammar School as they considered the education system far superior. With the imminent outbreak of the First World War, they took the boys back to the land of their birth to continue their education.

Gate Clock

The clock in question is that on the Greenwich Observatory, historically the most important clock in the world as it was used to signal the time to ships. Navigation of longitude required an accurate knowledge of time and without Greenwich Meantime this would never have been possible.

General Eliott

This 18th century military man is best remembered for leading the defensive campaign for Gibraltar against the Spanish from 1779 to 1783. On his retirement he was created Baron Heathfield.

General Sir Redvers Buller

At Crediton stands this establishment recalling the most famous local man. Born and died at the family estate in Crediton, this Victoria Cross recipient played important roles in the Anglo-Chinese War, the Egypt Campaign, the Anglo-Zulu War, and both the First and Second Boer Wars. Possibly, his full title would be a more fitting tribute to General Sir Henry Redvers Buller, noting his name should be pronounced 'Reevers'.

George

Unlike the Dragon previously, this undoubtedly does refer to England's patron saint. Whilst there have been six kings named George, the first four ruling in an unbroken line of 116 years from 1714, each king is either named specifically or, more often, referred to heraldically by the white horse.

George in the Tree

A public house at Balsall Common, in Warwickshire, which has a fairly complex history that begins with the former name of the pub, the Royal Oak. The story of the Royal Oak is told under its own entry, the sign of each is a variation on the theme of Charles II hiding in the Boscobel Oak at Shifnal, in Shropshire.

From here there are two possible explanations. One speaks of a former landlord, ignorant of the real origin, had the image changed to that of George III and produced the name. The second suggests the pub, having been renamed the George, lost its sign during an overnight storm. For months the sign was missing and, just when all hope of it ever being recovered had vanished, the autumn leaves falling from a nearby deciduous tree revealed it had been lodged in the upper branches all this time. Again, a seemingly plausible explanation for the name.

However, the second story fails to take into consideration the kings named George from the House of Hanover are rarely named but represented by the image of the white horse. Public houses named George refer to the patron saint of England and can be discounted. The same is true of the first explanation, which seems to be an example of creative etymology. Furthermore, there is no record of the place ever being named the George.

Oddly, the only thing that seems to be true of all these stories is the name George, which is common to them all. In an odd twist, the tree of the name could be referring to the large, and clearly aged, tree which once grew through the pub or, more correctly, the latter had been built around the tree – thus the Tree in the George would make a better name. This situation existed until at least the 1980s when it had to be removed as it was proving a very real danger to the structure.

Ghost Train

Another lesson in not taking a pub name literally for while we might expect to find a haunting behind this name, nothing could be further from the truth. Here is a tongue-in-cheek reference to a still controversial report of 1963 which resulted in the closure of thousands of miles of track and hundreds of railway stations. Whilst Richard Beeching may have seen these as unprofitable, the opposition is still seen in the name of a pub at Purton, in Wiltshire, where the old railway bridge is the only reminder of the train service.

Giddy Bridge

A Southampton pub which takes its name from the field known by the same name and marked as such on a 17th century map. Clearly, the name has been transferred to the field from a nearby river crossing. Today the name would suggest height and yet the topography does not support this. Hence it must have been a precarious river crossing, possibly just the trunk of a tree having fallen (or being deliberately felled) to create a 'bridge'.

Gig House

Nothing to do with music, this Wokingham pub stands on the site of the former factory of the Wellington Brewery. In days when distribution was all horse-drawn, the factory had its own stables and neighbouring storage space for the carts they pulled behind them. These carts were the 'gigs' and the parking space the gig house.

Gloucester Flying Machine

One of many pubs which refers to itself as a stop on the former coaching routes of our islands. For once, this is specific, a reference to the name of the service carrying passengers to the capital on three days of every week. As indicated by the pub's sign this was pulled by six horses instead of the usual four. Just as it is today, the greater the horsepower, the faster the journey. The service claimed it could reach London in two days which, considering the state of the roads and the 100 miles plus journey, is still impressive.

Goat and Compasses

Even if taken completely out of context, the unique language that produced the name of the Goat and Compasses can only refer to a pub. Typically with such apparently nonsense names there have been several suggestions as to its origins, the only link between them being they all agree there has been a corruption of at least one of the elements. The most common explanation suggests this began as 'God encompasseth us', this being entirely down to the 19th century novel *Framley Parsonage* where Anthony Trollope states this as the origin of this apparently meaningless name. Note this is a work of fiction and so is the explanation.

A second explanation accepts the 'Goat' and suggests this has exactly the same origin as the term 'scapegoat'. Many cultures once believed the goat to be a boon for any farmer to keep alongside other livestock, this suggesting it could well have its origins almost at the very beginning of farming. The very presence of the goat meant any ailments, misfortunes or bad spirits would be attracted to the poor goat, while the rest of the livestock could enjoy life to the full. In later years, a goat would be led around a house where sickness had taken hold for the same reason.

The real explanation is hardly so convoluted. As with so many pub names, the answer is heraldic, in particular the coat of arms of the Worshipful Company of Cordwainers. Examine the image and note the chevrons, quite easy to see as a pair of compasses used by many tradesmen including the cordwainers or leatherworkers, alongside the head of a goat. The earliest cordwainers used the hides of goats from Cordova in Spain, which is how they got their name and how the pub became the Goat and Compasses.

Gog and Magog

A fitting name for a Plymouth pub for their images are found cut into the chalk of Plymouth Hoe. They are mythical giants fought by a Cornish tribal hero and their story is found in many mythologies.

Gold Balance

A Kirkby pub named after a local vicar, the Reverend Thomas Wilkinson, buried in his own churchyard in the latter half of the 18th century. His life as churchman is less well remembered than his invention of the Gold Balance and the Pocket Balance, both used for weighing sovereigns.

SHEPHERD NEAME

THE GRANVILLE

Good Intent

At Aldington, in Kent, this public house recalls a schooner of this name which was known to be smuggling goods in and out of Kent during the 1830s.

Granville

Named after an 18th century Royal Naval vessel, itself taking the name of a French port known as 'the Monaco of the north'.

Great Harry

Great Harry was not a person but a vessel, the flagship of the navy built on the orders of King Henry VIII. Both the vessel and the pub were constructed at Woolwich.

Great Spoon of Ilford

A pub named from the 'spoon', a local term for a measurement of ale roughly equivalent to a quart. The 'great' is not specified but it is safe to assume it must have been a larger measurement. The establishment is on record as being one of the refreshment stops utilised by actor Will Kemp. In 1600 this character danced his way from Norwich to London, a distance of approximately eight miles which he covered in nine days.

Green Carnation

A green carnation was worn by Victorian gentlemen as a sign of their homosexuality. It is claimed this was a trend started by Oscar Wilde. While it is a matter of record this was Wilde's buttonhole of choice, whether he wore it first or simply followed the trend will never be known. What is clear, is the Green Carnation public house was named to honour the man of words who lived nearby.

Green Ginger

Slade and Son of Torquay, in Devon, once occupied this site. As the leading grocery store in the town they were able to negotiate a deal where they were the sole agent for Green Ginger Wine during the Victorian era.

JOHN
BARRAS
pub company

THE
GREEN MAN

Green Man

Some modern signs interpret this as a Robin Hood-like character dressed in Lincoln Green. However this is quite wrong and the Green Man is the mythical figure once synonymous with May Day celebrations. Sign painters depict the figure in so many ways, aside from the erroneous hero of Sherwood Forest, it is difficult to know who or what the Green Man was.

Ignoring the pub sign images for a moment, the most consistent depictions are found on churches and other traditional buildings not only in Britain but across Europe, Nepal, Borneo, India, Israel, Pakistan, Iran, and even Egypt. Clearly there is a very common idea here, this indicated by the very nature of the imagery which, other than in modern times, is confined to the face appearing from the plant world – be it tree trunks, leaves, vines, etc.

The Green Man has its basis in pagan culture and is probably best described as the male version of Mother Nature.

Guinea Pig

Maybe not the origin which first comes to mind but certainly a very creative pub name. This East Grinstead pub is not far from the Queen Victoria Hospital and its pioneering work on the treatment of burns by Sir Archibald McIndoe. This surgeon was determined to alleviate the suffering of the RAF and allied airmen whose role during the Second World War saw a high proportion of burns injuries. He requested volunteers be sent to his clinic where he used them to test his revolutionary techniques. It was not McIndoe but the test subjects who called themselves the Guinea Pig Club, although the surgeon was president until his death in 1960, since when the role has been filled by Prince Philip, Duke of Edinburgh.

Gunga Din's Colonial Inn

A name taken from the writings of Rudyard Kipling. Gunga Din was a soldier in colonial India, although it is unlikely most know anything but the last line: 'You're a better man than I am, Gunga Din'. Its choice is to advertise the product, for the poem does also contain the line: 'You may talk of gin and beer'.

Guss and Crook

An early mining term from when the smaller coal trucks were brought to the surface and pulled manually. The two terms respectively refer to the rope looped around the one pulling and the hooked part to which the rope is attached to the truck.

Gyngleboy

An early spelling which hardly makes much more sense when given as Jingleboy. Both are slang terms for a rich person, although it was also used for a coin. It is unclear which care first.

Half Moon

As depicted on the following image, pubs named the Half Moon are invariably depicted as our natural satellite at half phase. Yet this is nothing like the origin of the name which is actually heraldic. Families whose ancestors fought in the Crusades to the Holy Land would use the image to recall same. However, this is not a half moon but a crescent and should correctly be depicted lying on its back with the 'horns' pointing up.

Hangman's Tree

A Black Country public house with a story that goes back to 1840. This was the year George Smith was appointed as the assistant to William Calcraft, Staffordshire's official executioner. Within a few years he had taken Calcraft's position.

What the average Victorian considered entertaining would today be seen as morbid, gross, blood thirsty, or worse. Smith delighted in touring the pubs around the Black Country, where an ecstatic audience hung on his every word as he related details of his gruesome job. Just how good a narrator Smith was seems immaterial, he is known to have been of limited intelligence, as was his former boss and mentor, William Calcraft. Perhaps this was seen as a beneficial trait for an executioner.

That he had taken Calcraft's position so quickly was down to his predecessor's renowned incompetence, stories of bungled executions were plentiful. Not that George Smith performed any better. Both men favoured the short drop method, although by this time the long drop was considered preferable – the long drop breaking the neck being more humane than death by strangulation as a result of the short drop.

Smith's most notorious execution was that of William Palmer, the infamous Rugeley Poisoner. His extended death delighted the crowds but incurred the displeasure of the authorities – doubtless Palmer was none too pleased either. In later years, George Smith crossed the long arm of the law himself when money began to dry up. For years he had lined his pockets by selling pieces of the rope which hanged Palmer as mementos. He is said to have used an especially lengthy piece of for the purpose, although 30 yards seems a little extreme and created just to raise cash.

These facts seem to dispel local belief that the Hangman's Tree was named after the man who happily hanged the criminals until one day he was asked to dispatch his best friend. It was then he wrapped the noose around his own neck and committed suicide.

Hark to Bounty

At Slaidburn, in Lancashire, is this local pub with a delightful name only ever found in hunting country, a reference to the leaders of the packs of hounds.

Hart and Spool

A local pub name inspired by the locality. The Borough of Hersmere features a hart on its coat of arms, while the addition of 'spool' is a reminder of how important the film industry has been to the area.

Hatchet and Bill

At Yaxley, in Cambridgeshire, is a pub name featuring the two tools used in hedging; the hatchet needs no explanation while the bill is short for bill-hook which has a long blade with a hooked or concave edge.

Hautboy

This pub is named after an old instrument, the forerunner of the modern oboe. Created in France, and correctly called the hautbois meaning 'high wood', a reference to its pitch, when it crossed the English Channel it was Anglicised as 'hoboy', 'hautboit', 'howboye' as well as 'hautboy'. Any connection between the instrument and the pub in Ockham, Surrey, remains a mystery.

Hayling Billy

Named after the railway line serving Hayling Island from 1865 until 1963. This ambitious plan to build an embankment across the mudflats was initially served by a locomotive known as Puffing Billy, the name later transferred to the line. Today the line is a footpath and cycle route, while one of the later locomotives to work the line stood outside the pub from 1966. It is often said the engine was known as Hayling Billy but this is not the case.

Heilk Moon

One of the most unusual pub names in England, if only because nobody can agree on the meaning of the first word. What is agreed is this is from Cumberland dialect and describes a phase of the moon.

However, depending upon the source it could be a Full Moon, a Half Moon, or a Gibbous Moon (midway between the other two). If the Cumbrians cannot agree on the meaning the rest of the country have no chance.

Help Me Through This World

A Lancashire pub name which was once common throughout the land but which may well be unique today. The message is somewhat cryptic and has rather different explanations put to it. However, generally these all suggest the innkeeper has struggled through life to come thus far and would appreciate a helping hand – presumably in the form of your custom.

Hemlock Stone

Taken from a landmark near the pub in Wollaton, Nottinghamshire. This outcrop of rock is said to resemble the plant, despite the plant being green with white flowers and the rock made of red sandstone. Even in black and white the resemblance requires a leap of imagination.

Hen and Chickens

The sign outside this pub at Bisley, in Surrey, probably makes us think more of a meal than any of the real origins. Four centuries ago this was a name referring to the Pleiades, an open star cluster today more often said to be the Seven Sisters. A hundred years later it was used for the, once popular, plant found in almost every garden, London Pride. Then in Victorian times it was a kids' game. However, as a pub name it must surely refer to two sizes of pewter pots, the larger were 'hens' the smaller 'chickens'.

Hermit of Redcoats

The man in question is said to be one James Lucas. This local man could hardly be seen as a hermit in the traditional sense, for he hardly seems to have been devoted to any religion. His life changed in 1848 with the death of his mother. For the next 25 years he boarded himself up in his home and was never seen without a red coat until the day he died.

Hit and Miss

Found in several places across England, it is a comment by a landlord or owner on the random chance life throws at an individual. One example has seen the sign painters depicting the name as a cricket match, although the batsman appears to be trying to hit the ball with a golf club – some maintain this is meant to be the sport of hurling.

Holland Tringham

A Streatham public house remembering its most famous artist, Joseph Holland Tringham. This Victorian artist arrived here, having started his working life as an engineer, where his artistic talents shone through when he drew caricatures of his colleagues and superiors. He was sacked and moved to Streatham where he produced images of Streatham, copies of which are on display here.

Honest Lawyer

There are a handful of these around the country but we shall concentrate on that in Southampton. The sign features an obvious barrister figure but he is carrying his head under his arm. Clearly the message suggests the only way a lawyer can be honest is when he is dead. Some 200 yards away from the Southampton example is another, much newer, establishment which clearly was inspired by its rival as the sign proclaims this is the Bent Brief.

THE HOODENER'S HORSE

Hoodeners Horse

A delightful name which owes its existence here to Kent's most famous crop, hops. Hooding the hops refers to the process of drying them in the oast house. This was also the time when Morris dancers would use the hooden horse as part of their performance, a prop similar to the hobby horse.

Hook and Hatchet

To recognise a pub name without having to add the word 'pub' is actually quite simple to achieve. For example, in mentioning the George and Dragon or the Dog and Doublet our thoughts instantly turn to the public house. Just by linking two seemingly unrelated words with 'and' points to a pub name. If that means using the two most important words beginning with the same letter so much the better, for alliteration is still employed by advertisers. No product is mentioned in the phrases 'Flexible friend', 'Tiger in your tank', or 'Clunk, Click' and yet those of a certain age will recognise Access credit card, Esso petrol, and the seatbelt campaign, respectively.

In the Hook and Hatchet we not only have a pub name which uses alliteration, has two seemingly unrelated elements, but which was chosen for a very specific reason. At Hucking, in Kent, there are close associations with the Royal Navy and both hook and hatchet are found on the badge of a Chief Petty Officer Shipwright, probably an indication of an early landlord's previous career. These tools were not chosen arbitrarily, for they remind us the Royal Navy once had tree-felling rights and thus could obtain timber for building ships virtually anywhere they desired.

Hop and Kilderkin

A Bournemouth pub name featuring the crop famously used in brewing with an unusual barrel size from the Netherlands and not often used in this country.

Hope Tap

A pub built on the site of the former Hope Brewery. The addition of 'tap' refers to draught beers.

G W Horner's

Despite the locals always knowing this Chester-le-Street pub by its earlier name of the Fighting Cocks, it is correctly known by the town's benefactor who also owned the sweet factory. This was a major employer in the town until closing in the 1960s.

Horse and Chains

At Bushey, in Hertfordshire, is a name referring to the extra horses kept at the foot of Clay Hill. Fitted with special spiked shoes to enable them to get a grip, they were tethered to heavily laden wagons to assist in pulling these up this steep slope.

Hoy and Helmet

At Benfleet, in Essex, we find this name which could not exist elsewhere as it is based entirely on local terminology. A hoy was a small vessel used to carry passengers and cargo in and around the coast and the estuaries, the helmet is the local term for the jetty or quay.

Hufflers Arms

This Kent pub takes its name from they who ran shuttle services between the chandlers, traditional suppliers of ships' stores, and the vessels anchored offshore. The term 'huffler' probably began as a derogatory term for they were not licensed and would have been seen as unworthy of their cut by those who acted legally.

Humphrey Bean

Was the landlord of this Tonbridge pub when it was still known as the We Three Loggerheads, although for most of the 12th century this was a post office.

Hung, Drawn and Quartered

Found within a stone's throw of the Tower of London, the building was only built in 1914 when it was a part of Christ's Hospital School. The name is a direct quote from the writings of the most famous English diarist, Samuel Pepys. On Saturday, 13 October 1660 Pepys witnessed the first execution of the regicides, those brought to justice for the execution of Charles I. A plaque outside the building recalls Pepys' words describing how Thomas Harrison was 'looking as cheerful as any man could in that condition' as he approached the scaffold.

Huskisson

Named after the event, rather than the man, William Huskisson was the Member of Parliament for Liverpool who was invited to the opening of the Liverpool to Manchester railway on 15 September 1830. By no means the first demonstration of a railway locomotive, goods trains had been seen pulling loads in many places, this was important as it was the first of, what would be, a regular passenger service.

No less than eight trains departed together on that opening day. Huge crowds watched a long line of dignitaries headed by the Duke of Wellington, whose military career had ended and he was here in his role as prime minister. The prime minister's train ran on one track, the other seven travelling on parallel tracks, some ahead, others behind. It must have made for a memorable and quite splendid sight.

But these were early days and the day saw a number of problems. Firstly, one of the trains derailed and a following train ran into it. However, there were no casualties and, after a brief wait while the derailed locomotive was simply dropped back on to the rails, the delayed passenger service continued.

While it is only 35 miles between the two cities, the engines were scheduled a water stop. Staff advised the passengers it was only a temporary pause to take on water but around 50 of the dignitaries decided to alight and stretch their legs. William Huskisson was one of these and took the opportunity to seek out the prime minister, with whom he had fallen out publicly over several issues, and attempt to repair a few bridges.

It was whilst he was shaking the duke's hand he realised he was in danger for approaching him was the locomotive Rocket. Huskisson panicked and tried to scramble into the prime minister's carriage. He succeeded in climbing up but the door he was hanging on to swung open and left him dangling in the path of the oncoming locomotive.

William Huskisson lost his grip, falling in front of the engine and suffering horrendous injuries to his legs. The Member of Parliament for Liverpool died that evening and became the first passenger fatality associated with the railway network anywhere in the world.

I am the Only Running Footman

Once a servant ran ahead of his master's coach to clear the way, pay monies due at turnpikes, and even acted as a headlight at night by running ahead with a lit torch. As the 19th century dawned only one man was so employed, this the individual depicted on the sign, in the pay of William Douglas, the 4th Duke of Queensbury.

Ice Barque

A Grimsby pub named after the ships that brought ice from Norway to this port, ostensibly to keep the fishermen's catch fresh for longer.

Ice Wharf

Named for the adjacent ice wharf at Camden, built in 1837, to hold ice imported from Norway.

Isaac Merritt

Paignton, in Devon, was the home of Isaac Merritt, he made a small fortune mass-producing sewing machines under the Singer name.

Isonomy

Not simply an unusual name but a unique one. This Manchester pub was formerly the Grapes Inn but changed its name around the 1960s. The reason or inspiration for the change of name is unknown. However, it would certainly fit with the location and the clientele. Defining 'isonomy' we find a legal term referring to how the legal system sees everyone as equal, irrespective of gender, race, age, colour, culture, or religion. The catchment area would have produced a significant proportion of potential customers being either of Irish or Polish extraction, making this a fitting concept.

Ivory Peg

The name of Chelmsford is synonymous with the Roman occupation of Britain and the name of the Ivory Peg can rightly claim to be a direct result of this era of British history. This site had been home to the Bolingbroke and Wenley department store. When redevelopment brought the opportunity for archaeologists to excavate here, their efforts revealed a number of finds including the ivory peg from a musical instrument such as a lyre.

Ivy Tod

This may seem an odd name for a pub but both parts convey information. While ivy may not seem particularly relevant to a pub, it is used to show a connection to Bacchus, the Roman god of wine who wore a wreath made of ivy. However, here the reference is to 'ivy tod', a term used in Scotland for ivy and showing this establishment in London had a connection with north of the border.

Jack and Jill

This establishment, in Surrey, is named after the familiar nursery rhyme characters. It is told how they went up the hill to a well, and the pub does indeed stand on a hill and an old well was discovered in the area at the back of the premises when it was built in the 1950s.

Jack Fairman

In 1933 Jack Fairman opened a car showroom on this site in Horley, Surrey.

Jack in the Green

This is a name from the former May Day celebrations in this part of Devon. The 'Jack' being a boy, typically one employed by a chimney sweep. Hidden by a wooden frame covered with foliage he would walk about through those making merry on, what was always, one of the most important social days of the year.

Jack on Both Sides

This pub stood at a fork in the road, meaning it is a triangular building affording views on all sides. While location will have suggested this name, the real meaning behind this once popular phrase shows neutrality. Hence it seems the innkeeper was sending the message of this pub favouring no customers, irrespective of which direction they approached his pub.

Jack o' Lent

A pub in Midsomer Norton, Somerset, and a lasting reminder of a local story. Said story begins in the church dedicated to St John the Baptist – whose feast day coincides with Midsummer's Day and gave a name to the village. Here a tomb effigy, produced in Bristol in the first part of the 14th century, is thought to represent a member of the Gourney family, lords of the manor from shortly after the Norman Conquest.

His tomb no longer exists, destroyed when the church underwent a rebuild in the 18th century. The effigy was removed and placed in the garden at the neighbouring vicarage, where his career took a major downturn and especially as Eastertide approached. Here the stone image used to represent Judas, this most infamous baddie of the New Testament, was symbolically pelted with eggs and rocks. The latter explains why he is in such poor condition. That this happened at the end of the traditional period of fasting is why he, and thereafter the local pub, took the name Jack o' Lent.

Jack o' Newbury

A pub name that tells us where it can be found and recalls local man John Winchcombe, a 15th and 16th century wool merchant who spent a little of his considerable wealth to equip enough of his own men to form a small army to fight alongside Henry VIII against the Scots in 1513 at the Battle of Flodden Field.

Jack Phillips

Is a pub in Godalming, Surrey, named to honour the man who was cited as having saved more lives on board the ill-fated RMS *Titanic* than another individual – he was the wireless operator who stayed at his post sending out the call for help until the waters closed around him.

Jacob's Ladder

A name inspired by a biblical tale but not a connection to the church. Here the reference is the access to the Falmouth pub by 111 steps leading up the steep inclines of this ancient port. These were built by Jacob, not the patriarch of the Hebrews but Jacob Hamblen, a local builder, chandler and property owner who had the flight constructed to connect his property at the top with his businesses concerns at the bottom.

Jacob's Post

Strictly speaking, this public house is officially the Royal Oak. However, the sign subtitles the name as Jacob's Post. This seems a more relevant name for the local as it takes the name of the post that stands here, itself named after an important event in the history of Wivelsfield and Ditchling Common in Sussex.

Going back to May 1734, a Jewish pedlar, either Yacob Hirsch or Jacob Harris depending upon whichever record is consulted, murdered three people in the very pub that now depicts his name: landlord Richard Miles and his wife and their maid. He then stole money and clothing and fled. When the bloodied bodies were discovered Richard was just barely alive and, almost with his dying breath, identified his assailant.

Soldiers chased after Harris, pursuing him to the Cat Inn and on to West Hoathly. Here the murderer was discovered hiding in the chimney of Selsfield House, promptly arrested and thrown into a cell at Horsham Gaol. He was tried, found guilty and executed, his body then hung in chains at the gibbet on Ditchling Common, the remains of which is known as Jacob's Post.

But this was not the end of the story for the site later almost became a place of pilgrimage in the local area. The only remaining piece of the original post (a replica now stands here) is found within the pub, the rest has been pocketed in small pieces as it was said to be a cure for toothache and also, of all things, epilepsy. Even more morbidly, while the corpse still hung here women who were finding it difficult to conceive would visit and hold the hand of the murderer after which they would soon find they were pregnant.

Jackson Stops

This public house near Oakham, in Rutland, has a unique etymology. For many years this was the White Horse, but then the pub closed and remained so for some time. During its dry period all trace of the pub name, the brewery, and the beers vanished – indeed the only sign here was that of the estate agent – Jackson Stops.

Very soon, the original name had been forgotten and the community referred to it as the Jackson Stops. Amazingly, when the pub did reopen the locals petitioned the new owners to adopt the unofficial name and succeeded.

Jewel of the Severn

A reminder that Bridgnorth, in Shropshire, has been referred to as 'the Jewel of the Severn' by a number of writers.

John Barleycorn

Not a person but a humorous term for a beer or ale. Hardly, if ever, used today, 'he' is the subject of a folksong which humorously suggests that drink is the best friend of all and which says:

> Though the Hawthorn the pride of our hedges may be,
> And the rose our gardens adorn,
> Yet the flower that's sweetest and fairest to me,
> Is the bearded Barleycorn.
>
> Then hey for the Barleycorn,
> The Bonny Barleycorn,
> No grain or flower
> Has half the power
> Of the Bearded Barleycorn.
>
> Tho' the purple juice of the grape ne'er find
> Its way to the cup of horn,
> 'Tis little I care – for the draught to my mind,
> Is the blood of the Barleycorn.
>
> Then hey for the Barleycorn,
> The Bonny Barleycorn,
> No grain or flower
> Has half the power
> Of the Bearded Barleycorn.
>
> Tho' the Justice, the Parson and eke the Squire,
> May flout us and hold us in scorn,
> Our staunch boon friend, the best Knight in the shire,
> Is stout Sir John Barleycorn.
>
> Then hey for John Barleycorn,
> The merry John Barleycorn,
> Search round and about,
> What Knight's so stout
> As bold Sir John Barleycorn?

The name also appears in the writings of Robert Burns, Sir Walter Scott and Nathaniel Hawthorne, although not always seen in the same light but as the demon drink.

John Brunt VC

Once known as the Kent Arms, the John Brunt VC is the only pub ever named after a recipient of the Victoria Cross. John Brunt spent his formative years here in Paddock Wood, Kent, where he was known as a daring, mischievous and caring individual and this stayed with him throughout his military career. Following action in North Africa, he landed in Italy and was given command of a platoon. In December 1943, Lieutenant Brunt, with his platoon under heavy bombardment, crossed the river so many times in order to retrieve the wounded the men they called the river Brunt's Brook and he was subsequently awarded the Military Cross. Injury saw him sent back to Africa to recover, but soon returned to Italy where he rallied his men time and again to take the enemy's hold in the town where they were outnumbered by three to one. Under intense fire he sat on the turret of a Sherman tank and went from one position to another, rescuing his wounded and killing a great number of the enemy. His leadership, bravery and devotion to duty were beyond praiseworthy and would earn him the highest award bestowable in the British armed forces. Sadly, he never received the award as John Brunt was killed by mortar fire the next day.

John Jacques

The name of this Portsmouth pub remembers the days when this building was home to the Portsea Island Mutual Co-operative Society. Founded in 1873, at the end of the Second World War John Jacques took over the reins and led from the front for 20 years.

Johnny Todd

Not named after a person but after a folk song, albeit indirectly. The origin of the song, and indeed the lyric, depends upon which version we accept as the true version, for there is a link to Scotland, another to Belfast, and a third to the north of England. The latter is only known from Fred Kidson's 1891 publication *Traditional Tunes: A Collection of Ballad Airs* in which the author freely admits the printed version contained gaps when recited to him, gaps he had to 'fill up'.

Yet the lyric is not really relevant to the pub name, it is the tune that links it to this part of Liverpool. Many will still instantly recognise the signature tune to the long-running BBC television series *Z-Cars*, this officially known as Johnny Todd. This popular police series was set in this part of the city, also the reason it is still played before the start of the match at Goodison Park, home of Everton Football Club.

John Paul Jones

This inn is named after the so-called 'Father of the American Navy'. Born of Scottish parents his maritime career began at the age of 13 when he sailed out of Whitehaven aboard the Friendship as an apprentice bound for America. For the next eight years he voyaged many times across the Atlantic on a number of merchant and slaver ships but became disgusted with the cruelty of the slave trade. Eventually, now in command of his own vessel and almost 20 years after he had set sail on his maiden voyage, he returned to Whitehaven, this time he planned to lead an assault on the harbour. He planned to set the moored ships ablaze, but tide and an offshore wind slowed the progress of the two row boats and, although he reached the port, further problems beset them and their presence was revealed, allowing the townsfolk to foil the raiders.

John Russell Fox

In Hampshire, the *Andover Advertiser* was founded at this site in 1858 by John Russell Fox. Within ten years the newspaper had changed both premises and ownership but the pub remembers the original owner.

Jolly Taxpayer

The addition of 'Jolly' suggests an establishment of good humour, also linked to someone beginning to feel the effect of the alcohol. However, it seems the earliest use was as a synonym for 'very' or 'extremely', as is still used in such phrases as 'jolly good' or 'jolly lucky'. The location of the nearby Inland Revenue Office clearly had an influence here. Note that here the reference is specifically to the taxpayer, rather than the taxman, and thus doubtless a tongue was very firmly wedged in the proverbial cheek when naming this pub.

Juggs Arms

Locally, this is explained as a reference to the men who strapped baskets to their backs and carried the catch of fish from Brighton to Lewes. If this is correct we must assume this pub near Lewes was named for being a refreshment stop on the route.

Jumples

Jumples is seen as a place name a number of times around Yorkshire, as often appearing as Jumble as it does Jumple. Both refer to a hollow where a beck tumbles down into an overgrown area so as to appear to be swallowed up by the vegetation. However, it cannot be denied it also makes a good pub name.

Kicking Cuddy Inn

A Scottish dialect term is seen in this name, the northern counties have also been influenced by this reference to a donkey.

King and Castle

At Windsor, in Berkshire, this could easily be said to refer to the monarchy and castle found at Windsor. However, the origins are very specifically from the adjacent alleyway where the entrance features two images – a bust of Edward VII and an engraving of Windsor Castle.

King and Miller

A literary character, one told in song, is remembered by the King and Miller. When Henry II was lost in Sherwood Forest he came upon the miller who offered his hospitality in the form of venison. This could have resulted in the severest sentence as this was poaching the king's deer. However, the irony amused the king and the miller was knighted and henceforth known as Sir John Cockle.

King and Tinker

A similar story to the King and Miller and one also told in a ballad. Out hunting, King James I became separated from the rest of the party and called in at a local inn to await his courtiers. Within he got into conversation with a tinker, the latter speaking of his desire to know exactly what kind of man the king was. James replied this could only be known when everyone was hatless and such a cryptic comment could never be understood until the courtiers entered and immediately doffed their hats in the presence of the monarch. It was then he realised he had been speaking to the king himself.

King Canute

Once the story of the Danish king was well known, the tale of how he bragged he was so powerful he could even command the incoming tide to flow back from the shore. Of course, he could never accomplish this and when seated on his throne he succeeded only in getting his feet wet. Today, this story is not seen as the boasts of a monarch with a massive ego but, and this assumes it really did happen, one where a wise king is not impressed by those sycophants surrounding him and got his feet wet to prove them wrong.

Moving forward nine centuries a very high tide, an easterly wind and torrential rain combined to inundate coastal Essex in 1953 with the loss of more than 300 lives. As a reminder that nothing could stop the water, which came as far as two miles inland in the floods of 1953, the pub changed its name to the King Canute.

King Mark of Cornwall

A Newquay pub which draws on the association of Tintagel in Cornwall with the legendary Knights of the Round Table. Not that Sir Mark was a brave and virtuous individual, indeed the other knights saw him as untrustworthy and cowardly and set him up to reveal himself as such.

They spread a rumour that Sir Lancelot, the strongest and most formidable of Arthur's knights, was to dress himself up as the court jester in order to challenge and kill Sir Mark. This was not Lancelot but Dagonet, the real court jester, who appeared and challenged Sir Mark but he still believed the story he had heard and fled, hotly pursued by Dagonet and the rest of the knights.

Kings Fee

Hereford's history and its skyline are dominated by its cathedral. The area around the cathedral, and owned by same, was known as the Bishop's Fee while the remainder within the city's walls was the King's Fee.

Kings Head

Choosing the right name and sign are important when hoping to attract customers. Undoubtedly, the two most common choices are to show a patriot and a monarchist. Often these are general rather than specific references, such as the Kings Head at Mendelsham.

Kings Porter and Dwarf

A London establishment recalling two characters from the court of Charles I. The porter refers to William Evans of Monmouth, a porter to both Charles I and James I, who stood seven feet six inches tall. A contemporary account speaks of him as 'knock-kneed and splayfooted' and continues to describe how he would entertain the court with 'a little dance' which culminated in pulling the dwarf from his pocket. Evans died in 1634 aged just 35.

Said dwarf was Sir Jeffrey Hudson, a man of under four feet in height who was presented to Queen Henrietta Maria, consort of Charles I, at court as a seven-year-old boy when he emerged from beneath the crust of a large pie. The queen took to Jeffrey and, thereafter, he remained at court where he also became known as the Queen's

Dwarf or Lord Minimus. During the English Civil War he fought on the side of the Royalists and, following the execution of the king, fled to France with the queen. In France, he fell out of favour when a duel, where such had been outlawed, resulted in the death of his opponent.

His banishment from court signalled the start of a downward spiral. Within months he had been captured by Barbary pirates and spent the next 25 years in Africa in slavery. Eventually, he was one of those who were ransomed and brought back to England. At first he refused the offer of a return to the court of Charles II, but eventually relented and came to London where he was arrested and thrown into gaol as a Catholic and suspected as being involved in the Popish Plot. The next we hear of him is his release in 1680 and his subsequent death two years later. The circumstances surrounding his death are a mystery as is the location of a grave.

Kiss o' Life
A highly cryptic reference to the product. Here the reviving qualities of drink are advertised when the modern understanding of the phrase is artificial respiration.

Kittywitches
A name from one of the narrow alleys of Great Yarmouth. For a pub to take an existing local name is commonplace, the question here is as to the origin of the place name and there are a number of suggestions.

The narrowest of the town's alleyways, it tapers to just 27 inches at one end, one of a number of suggestions points to this being a family by the name of Wytche. Predictably, we also find a pointer to a coven of witches, although meeting here might prove a little cramped. Perhaps the best idea, although it is only a theory, refers its use as a local name for a crab. Those passing through this alleyway would need to edge through sideways, a characteristic trait of the crab or Kittywitch.

Knavesmire
As with the previous example, this is a place name, here that of the local racecourse. Whilst the 'mire' speaks for itself, we need to realise this was originally where the executions were once carried out, hence the addition of the first element.

Labour in Vain

Another example of sign painters distorting the meaning of a pub name, although here they can be excused. Irrespective of the creative image overhead, this began as a pointer to the quality of the product. In times when it was much more common to brew one's own, in the inn as much as at home, the name tells us it was no good attempting to match the quality of the beer found within.

Lad in the Lane

Undoubtedly, one of the oldest buildings in the city of Birmingham and one with a rich history worth examining. Many years ago, the author was enjoying a drink here when it was called *Ye Old Green Man*, a pub name which tells us it was used by the foresters working the estates of the Earl of Warwick. Over the years, the place has alternated between one name and the other, today it is the Lad in the Lane.

All those years ago, a regular customer informed the author that this was previously known as the Lad in the Lane. This is one of the many pubs in the land said to have an escape tunnel leading away from the building. Usually, the tunnel leads to a neighbouring church, another building which invariably has a room below ground level. Here, however, the tunnel was said to have led all the way to Aston Hall, a distance of almost two miles in a straight line and a highly improbable engineering feat. It was said it was in this tunnel that the young boy was murdered while attempting to escape, although from what and his identity is never mentioned.

Some years later, raising the subject brought smiles for none of the staff had ever seen any sign of a tunnel in the cellar and had clearly heard this question many, many times. One local remembered a cleaner, thought to be a little strange, for she was often found holding a conversation with nobody else in the room. One individual, who had no prior knowledge of her solitary conversations, asked who she was talking to and was told, "That lad."

Many stories have come out of these premises, not least that it is the oldest pub in Birmingham. Dendro-dating techniques – which enable archaeologists to accurately date when a piece of wood was cut – show the building dates from around 1386, yet we can be fairly certain it was a private house until the 1780s which makes it an old building, but not so old pub. Such an era makes it a candidate for a highwayman's haunt, here not said to be the ubiquitous Dick Turpin but a contemporary of his in Tom King.

It is difficult to see how a man who was accused of many crimes in the Essex and London areas could have been riding along the Chester Road for an ale in Erdington. The liaison between the two criminals is thought to have ended when King was captured and, in the struggle, was shot and died. Yet the shot did not come from his captors, but from the pistol of his supposed comrade just before making his escape, thus ensuring he could not be tempted or forced to give evidence against him. Thus, perhaps, the dark shape said to have appeared in the lounge here belonged to someone else.

La Marelle

A Glasgow pub that cleverly uses the French name for what British children would know as hopscotch. Whilst the name is clearly an advertisement for the products, adding 'hop', from which beer is brewed, to 'scotch', the spirit associated with Scotland, the game involves hopping or jumping into designated squares.

The modern idea of hopscotch takes the form of a line of single and double squares. Correctly known as 'courts' earlier examples are far more complex indicating these were not played exclusively by children. Records of the game being played in Britain date from the 17th century, although some point to this being brought to our shores by the Romans. These early players were known as Scotch-Hoppers for the game was then called Scotch-Hopper, as it was in the 1707 publication of *Poor Robin's Almanac* when we read 'Lawyers and physicians have little to do this month, so they may (if they will) play at Scotch-Hoppers'. The *Oxford English Dictionary* informs us a 'scotch' is used to refer to 'a line or scratch'. It is also known by other names to this day, regional names include 'hop-score', 'scotch hobbies', 'peevers', 'peeverels', and 'pabats'.

Lamb Inn

Another less than obvious religious pub name, here the reference is to Jesus Christ known as the Lamb of God.

Lambton Arms

A pub in Chester-le-Street remembering John George Lambton, 1st Earl of Durham, who served as British ambassador to Russia, Austria, then later Germany, before becoming governor-general of the British holdings in North America. There is also a Lambton Hounds at Pity Me, also in County Durham, recalling the earl's fondness for hunting.

Lamorna Wink

Two elements to this establishment in Cornwall, the address gives the answer to the first part for it is found at Lamorna Cove. The remainder is a reference to a winch, known as a 'wink' by local fisherman, used to raise the anchor at the bow of their vessels.

The LAMBTON
HOUNDS *Inn*

Land of Liberty, Peace and Plenty

At Rickmansworth, in Hertfordshire, this pub name is a reference to the nearby estate of Fergus O'Connor (1795-1846). O'Connor was a Chartist leader who advocated the so-called Land Plan, buying up tracts of land to be divided into equal smallholdings and let to individuals. His estate here was one such an example. Unfortunately, it was unworkable and, as effectively a lottery, was declared illegal and the estate sold off in 1857. Perhaps it was fortunate that O'Connor was unaware of the fate of his lands, for he had been declared insane some years earlier. Three years locked inside an asylum resulted in his death at the age of 61.

Lantokay

A very early name for what later became Leigh and, today, the town of Street in Somerset.

Last Drop

Found in several places in Britain, as a pub name it is easy to see why it is chosen as the drinks here are so good they will always be drunk to the last drop. However, the name may well have been inspired by a more macabre occasion, for many of these examples are near to where criminals were hanged.

Last Post

A public house in Beeston, Nottinghamshire, named because it had been the town's main post office.

Lazy Landlord

A Honiton pub named by the landlord whose job kept him busy from dawn until well after dusk and thought it a good joke to refer to himself ironically.

Leading Light

Faversham owed a lot of its 19th century development to Henry Weight, thrice mayor of the town. When he died in 1840, just yards away from these premises, he left money for schools, the recreation ground and almshouses.

LEATHERN BOTTLE

Leathern Bottle

Today we think of a 'bottle' as being made from glass – even the modern alternatives are always referred to as 'plastic bottles'. However, the idea of a glass bottle is a surprisingly modern concept and until Tudor times all bottles were made from leather and waterproofed with a covering of tar.

Ledger Building

Found in London's famous Docklands, the building had formerly been where the ledgers were stored recording the imports of the West India Docks.

Leg of Mutton and Cauliflower

At Ashtead, in Surrey, tradition has it the Leg of Mutton and Cauliflower has a connection to Epsom Race Course. Here the jockeys, owners and trainers would gather after one annual race to present the winner with the meat and the loser with the vegetable.

However, this tale seems to have been created to fit the name, for there is evidence in the form of a map to show the name existed in the 17th century before the first documented evidence of its use as a pub name. The map labels a local chalk pit with this name, undoubtedly this was coined to describe the shape of the workings. Some 50 years ago a group of men regularly met in, what is known as, the Red Room. It later transpired these were the conspirators in what became known as the Great Train Robbery.

Leviathan

A Watford establishment built in 1839. Erected to serve those who were travelling on the newly laid railway, it was inspired by the term used to describe the new form of transport, seen by some to be equated with the fearsome and unstoppable beast also known by this name. Any who think it may be linked to the beast itself may like to note the pub was known as the Leviathan Steamer for more than 30 years before reverting to its original name.

Linny

A humorous name suggesting that the public house in Honiton may a less substantial building than it really is. This is the local pronunciation of 'linhay', nothing more than what would be known as a lean-to shed, today.

Liquorice Gardens

At Worksop, in Nottinghamshire, the priory church was once known for the growing of liquorice in the gardens. The town's liquorice industry died out in the middle of the 18th century.

Little John

Hathersage, in Derbyshire, is held to be the last resting place of Robin Hood's right-hand man. A grave in the churchyard, marked by a 12th century tombstone, is documented as a plot of the Nailor, Naylor, or Nailer family (the spelling depending upon which record is consulted), this suggests he was born with that surname and that 'Little' was his nickname – other accounts give his birth name as

John Little. Whether this grave is the man, or if he even existed, can never be known but it is on record that this grave was opened in 1784, when a thighbone was removed. If the man had been of normal proportions this bone would mean in life he would have stood at around eight feet in height.

Live and Let Live

A pub name which is a political or social comment, although upon what depends on the location. The name is deliberately cryptic, hence the reason behind the majority of these 19th century names was deliberately hidden and will never be known. However, it might be as simple as the message ending the rivalry between an established pub and the newcomer.

Llandoger Trow

A Bristol pub dating from the 17th century which has many legends associated with it. Piracy and paranormal stories are the most often told, along with the idea that this was where Alexander Selkirk met author Daniel DeFoe and told him the story of his isolation on a desert island for four years, from which DeFoe produced his famous novel *Robinson Crusoe*. The pub is named after a trow, a kind of boat used in calmer waters to transport goods. In this example, we know both the specific boat and the owner, for it plied the waters around the Severn Estuary and the various tributaries bringing goods to the Welsh village of Llandoger on the River Wye. This vessel was registered to a Captain Hawkins.

Llawnroc

A public house we would expect to find in Wales, for it would fit perfectly with the idea of the Celtic tongue producing words beginning with what the English see as a double 'L' but is correctly a single letter. Less commonly, the name is also seen in Cornwall, for Cornish is a related language. Indeed, it is here in Goran Haven, near St Austell, the pub is to be found but this is no Cornish name, but simply a name created to appear Cornish for it is the name of the county spelled backwards.

Loggerheads

A pub that has actually given a name to the village of Loggerheads, which grew up around this pub. It is still the focal point of the village almost on the border of Shropshire and Staffordshire. This was once a surprisingly common name, indeed, in the 17th century, it was so well known even Shakespeare used it in *Twelfth Night*. The origin comes from a joke, where the sign showed two individuals with very obviously wooden heads above a caption reading 'We Three Loggerheads'. When anyone asked where the third loggerhead was, the response was to point at the questioner.

Long Stop

A pub name which is only ever found in places associated with our national summer sport of cricket. As a pub name it offers an invitation to enter, and stay, as long as one liked. When connected with cricket it is a fielding position, one never used in commentaries on the professional name but well known to schoolboys. Wicketkeeper is never one of the first places to be filled in the field, volunteers not only face every ball bowled, but retrieve every return from the fielders, and never drop the very hard cricket ball – it is a specialist position which few minor teams ever have the specialist to fill. Hence, the clever fielder, wanting to be in the action as much as possible, occupies a position immediately behind the wicketkeeper close to the boundary, thereby preventing a tremendous number of extras and filling the position of long stop.

Lord Arthur Lee

Named after the former MP for Fareham, later Lord Lee of Fareham, he left his former estate of Chequers in Buckinghamshire to future prime ministers as their country retreat.

Lord Denman

A Dagenham pub named after the former Lord Chief Justice of England. He lived at Parsloes in Dagenham for just two years from 1850. Suffering from ill health, he came here to rest and recuperate. His wife is buried in the local churchyard.

Lord Keeper of the Great Seal

Oadby, in Leicestershire, was where Sir Nathan Wright, Lord Keeper of the Privy Seal was lord of the manor.

Lover's Leap

A name found in several places in Britain, but in just two places as a pub name. The best known story is found in Middleton Dale, Derbyshire, where the jilted Hannah Baddeley jumped to end her own life in 1762. However, she survived the 80 foot drop with just a few cuts and bruises but, according to the parish register, was buried just two years later aged 26.

The second narrative is from Yorkshire, where Kirkby Overblow has a Lover's Leap public house. Listen to locals and they will regale you with various versions of the story of the broken-hearted woman who leapt from Almes Cliffe. Again the woman survived, having her fall halted when her crinoline dress acted as a parachute and brought her gently to the ground. They will also tell you this is the reason for the place name of Kirkby Overblow. Perhaps the pub should be renamed the Gullible Inn.

Luck Penny

A Stafford pub inspired by the livestock market tradition of the seller returning a penny or two to the buyer, both would thereafter enjoy good fortune. The pub name should be seen as an introduction, one where the lucky pennies could be spent.

Mad Cat

At Pidley, in Cambridgeshire, is a name derived from its sign. Landlords would do anything they could to save money, as indeed will any good businessman, and one of their biggest investments hung outside in all weathers advertising the premises. Hence it is understandable why they may be tempted to take up a patron's offer to paint something in exchange for a few liquid freebies. Unfortunately, this led to a number of sub-standard signs and, perhaps, this is one of many examples.

It seems the image should have been that of the heraldic White Lion. However, the locals were less than impressed and began referring to both sign and pub as the Mad Cat and the landlord promptly adopted the name.

Maes Knoll

A pub named after a nearby feature. Maes Knoll is a hill-fort built about 250 BC by the Dobuni tribe. It was not named by these Celts, this is an Old English name from maerc or 'boundary'.

Magnet and Dewdrop

To unite two seemingly unrelated items is seen as the classic pub name. However, here the two items are related in them both being invitations, where the 'magnet' would attract the customers, while the pun is clear for a 'dewdrop inn'.

Mallyan Spout Hotel

As locals of Goathland will tell you, this place in the North Yorkshire Moors is named after a local waterfall.

Man in the Moon

A name with no connection to the perceived face created by lunar seas, although this may have been the source of the original story. Examine the sign and it shows a man gathering sticks. This points to a tale told many times from various sources, including the Bible where the man was stoned to death for disobeying the fourth commandment by working on the Sabbath. Thereafter the story departs from the biblical version by telling how he was deprived of every sun-day (Sunday) thereafter by having his image etched into the moon and thus an eternity of moon-days (Monday). The hole in this story is that Sunday is not the Sabbath in the Jewish faith, which is relevant to the Old Testament, but is Saturday.

Mannamead

Plymouth, and the area known as Mutley Plain, was developed by the company Ellery, Fowler and Bennett. This particular name comes from two fields here, East Mannamead and West Mannamead.

Margaret Catchpole

With the sign depicting a struggle between smugglers and the men from the revenue, the inn named the Margaret Catchpole would seem to be unrelated. However, walk around and we find this is one of those rare signs with different images on each side. Here we see the eponymous character on a horse at a good gallop and a reminder of a heroine from Suffolk folklore. Margaret is said to have fled to London for a rendezvous with her lover, smuggler William Laud, dressed as a sailor. However, the horse was stolen and she was sentenced to death for the crime. This was later commuted to transportation to Australia, where she arrived in 1801. Her life in the antipodes is well documented, for she chanced to marry a man of good standing and became well respected. Interestingly, the origin of her maiden name rather conflicts with her life in England. Catchpole is from the Old French cachepol meaning 'an officer of the sheriff'.

Marine Grotto

Something of a recluse, Peter Allan was born in 1799 to a local shoemaker and his wife. He grew up fascinated by the quarries in the area and as soon as he was old enough began to carve the limestone cliff into, what became known as, the Marsden Grotto, named after Marsden Bay. Single-handedly this man carved out no less than 15 rooms which connected to a farmhouse and tavern on the cliff top. He is often spoken of locally as 'the hermit', for he rarely left the cave system, but Peter Allan was simply an eccentric who preferred the company of his wife and eight children. The mayor did not approve of the man or his life and attempted to evict him, claiming he did not own the land at the cliff top and, therefore, he was not the true owner of the caves beneath. The case was overturned but Allan died in the following year of 1849. Erosion caused the cliff face to collapse in 1865 but the caves and the pub above remain, with access via a lift from the surface.

Marlipins

A pub in Sussex which, along with the Marlipins Museum, recall the board game played from around the 14th century, correctly known as merels. It derived its name from the French for the token with which the game is played. It is also known by other names such as miracle, moral, marl, Nine Men's Morris, and Fox and Geese.

Marlow Donkey

For 65 years a small tank engine worked the branch line between Marlow and Reading, passengers being welcomed by the Railway Hotel. When steam was replaced by diesel in 1962 the Railway Hotel changed its name to the Marlow Donkey, as the branch line engine had been affectionately known.

Marrowbone and Cleaver

A pub that was originally in the area known as the Butchery, later Queen Street, thereafter revived as the brewery still liked the name. The sign features a butcher banging a cleaver with a shank bone, a traditional Tudor custom where a line of butchers' boys would use cleavers of differing sizes and thus get a tune-like peal out of them to accompany the newlyweds as they left the church.

Masqued Haunt

A London pub named after the nearby gatehouse of the Priory of St John, it later served as the office of the Master of the Revels. Responsible for licensing entertainments such as drama, music and dance, the masque being a lavish production performed by masked figures.

Mermaid

There are a number of pubs known by this name, many of which are located near the coast. However, the one that has the most interesting story to tell features the image of the fabled female brushing her hair and is sitting alongside Blackmere Pool, near Leek in Staffordshire.

The ridge of land high over the town of Leek seems an odd location for an almost perfectly circular body of water some 50 yards across. This answer to the name is said to be found below the surface of these very dark waters in one of the strangest stories to emerge from the county. Not only is Blackmere Pool over 30 miles from the sea, it is over 1,300 feet above it. It is rather surprising to find it to be the traditional home of a mermaid. Every night at the stroke of midnight she rises to the surface to comb her long hair. Anyone wandering past at this late hour and who is seen by her will be dragged down into the cold, deep waters.

Miner's Standard

This pub near Matlock is a reminder of the many mines that pepper the Peak District. This refers to the standard measuring dish for lead ore, in use since at least the 16th century.

Molly Millar

Often said to be named after a Wokingham beauty, the daughter of an 18th century landlord, nothing could be further from the truth. Whilst there was a lass called Molly who rejected every gentleman who came to court her, dying a spinster in 1766 at the age of 67, she was Molly Mog, a woman immortalised by the poem subtitled 'The Fair Maid of the Inn'. Molly Millar did live in Wokingham, there is also a road named after her. Yet she is not remembered for her beauty, Molly Millar's infamy was a result of her reputation as a witch.

Montagu Pyke

In London's West End, specifically Charing Cross Road, is this building named after the man who designed the building as a cinema.

Morning Star

A name that seems to have caused some confusion for the sign painter has depicted this as a celestial body, this being the alternative name of the planet Venus. However, it does seem more appropriate for this to refer to a famous steam engine built by Robert Stephenson for the Great Western Railway.

Mortal Man

Originally, this was known as the White House but acquired its present name, first as a local reference, following a stay by painter Julius Caesar Ibbetson. So impressed was he by the innkeeper's hospitality he painted a scene inspired by the following verse:

> Oh mortal man that lives by bread,
> What is it makes thy nose so red?
> Thou silly fool, thou look'st so pale,
> 'Tis drinking Sally Birkett's ale.

Within a few short years of the sign being erected the name of the place had officially become the Mortal Man.

Moth and Lantern

Until the 1980s this was the Grenville Arms, then a change of management saw a competition to find a new name. Moth and Lantern was chosen as it reflected both the pub and its customers, the latter being attracted by the former in both cases.

Mother Huff Cap

In recent years, this name has been changed to the Huff Cap Inn, a name which is closer to the original meaning. The phrase may not be understood today but in the 16th century everyone would have understood how a drink could 'huff one's cap', much as a drink could 'go to one's head' today. Hence, this is a warning to drink in moderation, albeit one which is more than 500 years old.

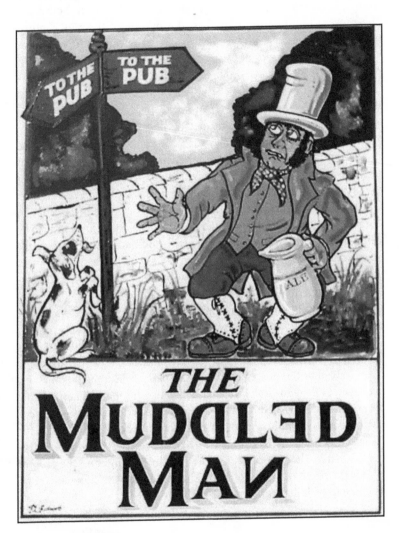

THE
MUDDLED
MAN

Muddled Man

Surely, one of the most endearing pub name etymologies in the county, if not in the country, is found at Crewkerne, in Somerset. The present building dates back to the middle of the 17th century when it was a weaver's cottage, it was not for another 150 years that it first became licensed premises, for the sale of beer and cider only. At the time it was not the only pub in the parish, the Half Moon was further along the road and hence it was 'the newer inn'. In the 1960s the Half Moon closed and it was around this time the local council wielded their pedantic pen and decided all pubs that did not offer accommodation could not call themselves inns. Hence a change of name was required for, unlike other inns, it couldn't simply drop this element, as this would then have simply been the 'New'. Looking to a local point to point racehorse, which ran the West Chinnock to Chisleburgh steeplechase course, the pub was renamed after the horse and became the Salamander and stayed as such until the 1970s when a new landlord was unhappy with the name. Trying to think up a new name for anything is never as easy as it sounds and pubs are harder than most. To add to the landlord's woes his wife had been admitted to hospital and he was left to look after the home, the pub, his young family and, worst of all, the accounts. In the days before home computing the company books were just that, books in which credits and debits were entered by hand. In public houses this function was inevitably the task taken on by the landlady, so when the poor man arrived at the hospital with all the paperwork one evening and managed to drop the lot in a heap on the floor, his wife exclaimed how he was such a 'muddled man'. A passing nurse, who had come to know them, remarked on how well-suited this would be as a pub name, for it also aptly described most men when they were just a little the worse for the drink. The brewery agreed to the name change and the present sign is the result of a competition held to redesign the sign which had become tatty. It depicts the name perfectly well.

Mystery

A strange name with an even stranger origin. It was renamed when Southsea's harbour area was completely redeveloped leaving only this public house untouched. Just how this happened was a mystery.

My Father's Moustache

Almost every sign will depict a gentleman with an impressive handlebar moustache. It will probably come as no surprise to discover that facial hair has no connection with the origins. Around the early part of the 20th century the phrase 'Your father's moustache' was used to deride anyone who was thought to be spinning a yarn – although just where this came from is a mystery. It seems the change to 'My' is saying 'You won't believe it' and yet another way of saying this is an exceptional public house.

Mytton and Mermaid

Alliteration is a powerful marketing tool and was recognised as such many years ago. Pub names can also quite obviously be nothing else when two seemingly unrelated items are linked. Furthermore, locals of a small community like to see it play some role in the new name. All three factors are satisfied here, while producing a decent story behind the name.

The man in question was Sir John Mytton, the local squire who died in 1834. His interest in the maids of the local village of Atcham is almost legendary; indeed the name is a play on 'mere maids', all that Sir John was interested in. He is shown on one side of the sign holding a foaming tankard of ale, with the mermaid emerging from the brew. Turn the sign around and see the story from the maid's viewpoint, where the mermaid is combing out her long hair and staring at the mirror in which we see Mytton wearing the most lecherous of grins.

Nelson Arms

Named as one of Britain's greatest ever heroes in a poll of 2002, the name of Lord Nelson adorns more pubs than any other individual. Invariably remembered for his victory at Trafalgar in 1805, his naval career began in 1770 at the age of 21 and included many other fine victories and campaigns.

Never Turn Back

A lasting tribute to the brave volunteers who man the lifeboats and one, in particular, is found in the name of the Never Turn Back at Caister-on-Sea in Norfolk. A severe gale notwithstanding, the crew launched to aid a ship in distress. In 1901 there were no state-of-the-art technology vessels like we see today and, when the lifeboat capsized, many of the lifeboat crew were lost. At the resulting inquest the coxswain was asked why they did not take the clear choice of returning to shore. His reply gave the name of the pub when James Haylett replied: "Caister men never turn back, Sir."

Nevison's Leap

A pub in Pontefract associated with the famed highwayman, Swift Nick, otherwise known as William Nevison. This was named to mark the prodigious leap said to have been accomplished by the criminal in order to escape capture. In truth, his horse will have made the leap, not caring one jot whether his rider had been apprehended or not. Doubtless the story has been embellished over the years much as that of another highwayman, Dick Turpin and his famous ride from London to York on his horse, Black Bess. Turpin was hanged outside York and, we are told, buried with his horse in a grave at Fishergate, York. Many doubt whether Turpin is actually here, and Black Bess most certainly is not for his famous horse and he had parted company some years earlier.

It will come as no surprise to find the Turpin story is entirely fictitious, 200 miles in a single day for any horse (other than the winged horse Pegasus from Greek mythology) is quite impossible. Yet the story had been told many times before Turpin was even born. Daniel Defoe, writing about his tour of Britain in 1727, told of William Nevison riding from London to York 50 years earlier to establish an alibi and remove himself from suspicion of a crime he certainly committed. This became established in folklore, as it probably had been even before Defoe put pen to paper, and was never attributed to Turpin until 1867 when William Harrison Ainsworth wrote a serialised and fictitious account in the popular Victorian publications known as penny dreadfuls.

NoBody Inn

This old cottage at Doddiscombsleigh, in Devon, dates from the late 16th century. One origin of this name is depicted on a plaque on an exterior wall, where a gentleman is seen knocking on the door. Clearly, the message here is there is no response as, presumably, there is no one within. However, this name comes from the 19th century and this explanation followed. Both are as credible as the idea this was named from the image on the sign depicting just a face – ie there was no body. In truth, the name was undoubtedly coined to be humorous.

Nodding Donkey
A reference to those 'nodding' pumps on oil wells, several of which stood nearby when this pub opened 30 years ago.

Nont Sarah
A former landlady was known as Aunt Sarah, which is the correct pronunciation of the pub now known as Nont Sarah.

Noughts and Crosses
A property in Polperro that opened as a pub as recently as the 1960s. However, the property began as two cottages built around the end of the 16th century. During the interim period it found several uses, for much of the time as a bakery. When a certain woman was running the bakery she got into the habit of marking sold loaves with a nought, adding the cross when paid for. It may have been a simple accounting system but it made for an excellent pub name.

Nowhere
According to the management of this rather eccentric public house, the name was coined deliberately to provide the perfect alibi for the hen-pecked husband. When his wife demanded to know where he had been, he could truthfully answer, "Nowhere."

Nut and Bolt
Yattendon, in Berkshire, was the home of this pub formerly known as the Axe and Compass. It changed its name when licensees John and Val Bolton came here and it is generally believed their surname suggested itself as the new name.

Observatory

An Ilkeston pub that remembers the first Astronomer Royal, John Flamsteed, was born nearby.

Ock 'n' Dough

A name chosen from a number of suggestions by the locals. Just after the Millennium celebrations had ended, the new pub was opened and named for a traditional local delicacy. This consists of a pork hock (or 'Ock) with potatoes in a vegetable stock which, when baked in a pie, produces a soft pastry (or 'Dough') base with a crisp top crust.

Oily Johnnies

Locals used to enjoy a glass at the Oak Tree, such a tree still stands at the front of the building in Winscales, Cumbria. In June 2008, the name was officially changed to Oily's, although locals had known the place as Oily Johnnies for many years. The name referred to a gentleman by the name of Johnnie who used to sell paraffin oil from here.

Old Bill and Bull

In the Yardley district of Birmingham, on the opposite side of the road from here, for a long time stood the Bull's Head public house. When that closed a new pub opened here, using the former police station as a base.

Old Clink

The building was erected in 1851 at a documented cost of just £60. It comprised two cells, used principally for the local drunks and vagrants, whilst above were offices for parish officers and overseers. Within 15 years the building had been replaced by the local police station and the original fell into disrepair. Today, it has been renovated and houses offices. Perhaps some of those who work here cross the road to the public house opposite which now bears the name of the Old Clink.

Old Crutched Friars

A pub which takes its name from the street, itself a name listed as Crutched Friars and was, in 1405, recorded as Crouchedfrerestrete where the origin of 'the street of the Friars of the Holy Cross' is quite easy to see.

Old English Gentleman

Clearly, the sign and the name are an advertisement and here that message relies on everyone considering themselves a cut above the rest and a true gent. Having sowed the seed of an idea the pub instantly offers a place for the gent to imbibe.

Old Fourpenny Shop

What was once the Warwick Tavern, in Warwick, was renamed to reflect the history of the place. When those working on bringing first the canal, and, later, the railway to this ancient town, they were able to come here to select from a range of products to fuel and refresh them, all at a cost of fourpence. This was, of course, pre-decimal pennies when there were 240 pennies to the pound.

Old Guinea

This pub at Potters Bar, in Hertfordshire, is certainly named after the former gold coin, a denomination still used in the buying and selling of race horses where it is equal to 21 shillings (£1.05). Yet the first guinea was stated to be equal to a pound, the term 'guinea' referred to the coin, not the value. However, soon the value of gold – these were minted using gold extracted by miners in the West African country of Guinea, hence the name – meant the gold content made the coin worth more than its face value. Not only did this result in the increase in valuation but is also the reason for the name of the pub, a suggestion the real worth of this place is more than it appears at face value.

Old Harry

A pub in Poole, Dorset, named to refer to three chalk formations, a part of the Isle of Purbeck and marking the eastern end of the famed Jurassic Coast. Of the three we see a stack known as Old Harry and a former stack, now eroded to a stump, known as Old Harry's Wife. Legend has given these rocks a name, although whether 'Old Harry' is a pointer to the Devil (he is said to have slept here) or to the infamous local pirate Harry Paye is unclear.

Old Hat

A visit to the local pub will reveal the sign of the Old Hat, which does not mean something which is old-fashioned as is understood by the phrase today. This indicates this was a meeting place for the Old Hats' Club, founded in 1777 and who were the first to follow the sport of pigeon shooting.

Old House at Home

A pub name remembering a ballad popular with soldiers serving abroad. The ballad speaks of a mother and her son, both remembering how content they were in younger times.

Old Jack

A Shropshire pub built as a coaching house in the 1830s. However, the name is much older and refers to a leather beer jug, one with metal rings at top and bottom to give it stability and then sealed with tar, to produce a drinking vessel. Normally these were rather earlier than the 1830s but here it refers to a specific item, one lined with horn and silver mounting which was kept at the pub. The upper band was inscribed with the words 'Jack of Corra is my name; don't abuse me then for shame', while on the lower band could be read 'From time immem-orial'. Holding an approximate pint it was last seen hanging in the pub in 1860 and has never been seen since.

Old Mint

A pub occupying a 14th century stone building, originally a hospice. That this is made of stone is the main reason it has survived to the 21st century, comparatively safe from the fires which have ravaged the town of Southam, in Warwickshire. Note this place has never officially been where coins were minted but comes from it being a collection point for silver donated by noblemen during the English Civil War. Such was subsequently melted down and the coins used to pay the soldiers who fought at the Battle of Edgehill in 1642.

Old Parish Oven

A name derived from the former building on this site. Here stood a large oven, the door of the former oven was incorporated into the fireplace when the pub was built in the 1970s.

Olde Peculiar

A name which is most likely to be shown as Old Peculier owing to this also being the name of an ale brewed by Theakston's. As the Armitage establishment is a Theakston's house this is the origin of the pub name – albeit many of this, and similarly named houses, will insist it is a comment on the locals!

Old Rectifying House

Once an excellent name for a pub for it advertises a place where purified water was produced. An important commodity in times when it made more sense to drink ale than water.

Old Roof Tree

A farmhouse near Morecambe where one building was known as Roof Tree Cottage. Named for where a branch of a tree had grown right through the roof. When the building became a public house, the rebuild kept those parts of the tree embedded in the fabric of the new building, and the pub was named as we see it today.

Old Sal

At Longton, in north Staffordshire, where the pub invited those associated with the local colliery to drink by naming the pub from the nickname of the colliery.

Old See-ho
A Gravesend pub which is a variation on the name of the Hare and Hounds. Just as the cry of Tally-Ho went up when the riders spotted the fox, so See-Ho when up when the greyhounds were loosed upon the hare.

Old Success Inn
The pub points out it is an old fisherman's pub and refers to it being where men were hired by the Pilchard Seine Net Company, bringing prosperity to the village. However, other locals point to this being where the Transatlantic Cables came ashore and were linked to the communications network on the land.

Old Thirteenth Cheshire Astley Volunteer Riflemans Corps Inn
A name with a military theme, overlooking Stalybridge, and created to produce the longest pub name in England.

One and Three
An early example of the modern idea of using the number on the postal address for the premises as the name. However, as the number 13 is seen as unlucky, the name was changed to represent the two single digit numbers individually.

Open Arms
In pub names 'arms' is generally used to mean 'pub'. Of course no pub is of much interest until it is open – but it is together where they create a welcoming name.

Ostrich Inn
Has claims to be the third oldest inn in England. Founded in 1106, the building was originally known as the Hospice but, over the years, this became corrupted to Ostrich. The place is reputed to have been the site of more than 60 murders, many of which were down to the Jarmans, landlord and landlady in the 17th century. It seems they had hooked up a winch to the bedstead and thus could open a trap door and allow the sleeping rich guest to slip out of bed and into a vat of boiling liquid below.

Other Side of the Moon
During the 1950s and 1960s space exploration was attracting tremendous interest. This pub was opened shortly after the first successful launches and named to commemorate such.

Ounce and Ivybush
At East Grinstead, in West Sussex, is this reminder of the Sackville family, former landowners here.

Owd Betts
Named after a former landlady and the local dialect for 'Old Betty'.

Oxnoble
A Manchester pub named after a potato, a popular variety in the northwest of England.

Packet Station

This name recalls the post office naming Falmouth as a port dealing with overseas mail – in short a packet station. Thereafter, the Falmouth Packets were constructed, a fleet of fast ships, lightly armed and captained by men who were acclaimed as heroes. Falmouth remained the leading packet station until the end of 19th century.

Pack of Cards

Visit this pub, on the north Devon coast at Combe Martin, and the name will not be immediately apparent. However, spend time looking at this white building and you will begin to unravel the name coined by the local squire when he ordered the building to have four floors, 13 doors, and 52 windows. Whilst not named until his death in 1716, they were designed to reflect four suits, 13 cards in a suit, and 52 cards found in a pack of cards.

Panniers

Standing in Butcher's Row, Barnstaple, where more than 30 outlets sold meat. The panniers were the wicker baskets in which the traders carried their expertly butchered carcasses for sale.

Papermakers Arms

As a pub name, the Papermakers Arms seems to be nothing more than a trade name, and one of particular popularity in Kent. However, it is also true to say landlords are well known for the subtlest of messages on their signs and, together with the humour of pub names, perhaps there is a hidden comment here. In the earliest days, when paper was made by hand, a slurry of wood fibres and water was scooped up in a wire frame and shaken to ensure the thin film was evenly distributed and thus, when allowed to dry, would produce a sheet of paper of uniform thickness. As a result the papermakers were instantly recognised because their hands would constantly shake and perhaps this is the reference to their 'arms' here.

Parchment Makers

A pub in Havant remembering how this town was renowned for the quality and purity of its parchment.

Parkstone and Heatherlands

Occupying the former Co-Operative store in Bournemouth, the pub takes the name of the original co-operative, the Parkstone and Heatherlands Society, both earlier place names.

Parson and Clerk

Streetly's parson and squire quarrelled vociferously and, even, violently towards the end of the 18th century. Eventually, the matter was settled in court when the squire was victorious. He used his considerable influence to erect a statue on top of the local pub, then known as the Royal Oak. He ordered two figures be carved: one, the parson, was depicted with head bowed in prayer, the second, his clerk, stood above and behind him ready to swing the axe. The pub name was changed to mark the dispute and its amusing conclusion.

Paul Pry

The *Paul Pry* is the name of a play written by John Poole. First produced in 1825, the eponymous character is forever interfering in the lives of others. The play proved extremely popular and toured the land for some time. Perhaps the pub sign featuring a man listening at a door marked 'Private' is a copy of the poster used to advertise the play at the local theatre in Peterborough.

Peep o' Day

A Worcester public house with a name that has a number of possible origins. The most obvious describes the first rays of dawn, and while sunrise is used for some establishments this does not seem particularly appropriate here. Neither does it seem likely to be a reference to the alternative name for the Star of Bethlehem plant, any more than the religious reference of a book by a Mrs T Mortimer in 1836 where the subtitle (an obligatory addition at the time) read, 'A series of the earliest religious instructions the infant mind is capable of receiving'.

The most likely explanation is that of the Peep of Day Boys, not quite the angelic figures the name might suggest. These were men allied to Protestant orders who searched the homes of known Catholic families at dawn searching for arms, a continued watch on their Christian rivals following the Gunpowder Plot.

Peggy Bedford

The lady herself was the licensee in the Victorian era, when the pub was known as the Kings Head.

Pennsylvanian

The American state was founded by William Penn, hence the name. Penn not only lived at Rickmansworth, but is buried at the Friends Meeting House in nearby Jordans.

Pennycomequick

A Plymouth public house and a former place name. When we learn the name meant the same as it appears to as a pub, ie the land was profitable, its choice is easily understood.

Penny Gill

A public house in Spennymoor, Co Durham, taking a local place name. A 'gill' is an Old Scandinavian word describing 'a deep narrow gorge', however, the first element is more problematical. It certainly has no link to currency but may come from the name of a family once resident nearby. However, most likely this comes from an oxymoron, for a valley invariably stands alongside a high point or penn.

Peveril of the Peak

The name of a coach that ran from Manchester to London and back. The name of Peveril can be traced to William de Peverel, a son of William the Conqueror, who was given Nottingham Castle by his father shortly after 1066. His name was, in turn, taken by Sir Walter Scott for his novel *Peveril of the Peak* published in 1823. Here the title character is Sir Geoffrey Peveril, a descendant of William the Conqueror and set in the days of Charles II.

Phantom Coach

An old coaching inn, which was the terminus for a route between Cheltenham and this establishment in Coventry. It is said, one coach left the Coventry pub one night, nothing unusual in that other than neither it, nor any of the passengers, was ever seen or heard of again.

Pig and Tater

At Guildford, in Surrey, one unique name was the Pig and Tater. It was always known as the Forester or Foresters, reverting to its original name quite recently, but to the locals this is the Pig and Tater. It is said this came from a group of regulars who, having worked their allotments where all they grew was potatoes and allowed herds of swine to roam when these crops had been lifted, spoke of nothing else when coming to the (then) Foresters and all the talk of 'pigs and taters' resulted in the name.

Pig and Whistle

This has become very popular over the last two or three decades yet its origins have never been adequately explained. The phrase 'pigs and whistles' is found in the *Oxford English Dictionary* with examples cited from as early as 1681, it being used to refer to something gone to ruin and habitual visits to inns would have been seen as certain ruination. There is also a Sussex pig, a drinking vessel shaped like the head of the animal and used to 'wet one's whistle'. Or perhaps this is a corruption of 'peg and wassail', a supposed salutation wishing a measure of health, today we would say 'cheers'. One early example claims it came to be used by merchant navy men when they retired and set up at an inn, although the claim that all galleys in merchant ships were known as the pig and whistle is unsubstantiated. Whatever the origins, if there actually is one, it is true to say the name lends itself very easily as a pub name. Two apparently unrelated items linked by 'and' is the typical form for a pub name.

Pigeon Pair

This pub at Kingswood opened as the Station Hotel but renamed as the Pigeon Pair when refurbished in 1968. A link between Kingswood and pigeons began with an early involvement with Reuters News Agency. Brought to the town by train, the pigeons carried news messages faster than other methods and much cheaper than telegrams. The 'pair' may have been twins associated with this venue, one male and one female, the usual clutch laid by a breeding pair of pigeons. Tradition maintains the brood is always two eggs, one of each sex, but there are rare examples of three eggs.

Pigs

Often a pub sign recognised as being heraldic or partly so, has an origin lost in history. One would imagine the lord of the manor would be honoured to see his arms hanging outside the local pub but not in the case of Edgefield in Norfolk and landholder Lord Bacon. When the landlord wanted to display these arms outside the Bacon Arms he categorically refused to give permission. Undeterred, the landlord amended the name to the Three Pigs, devising his own sign where the trotters of the three were joined. Today, the sign has but two pigs, while the name has changed yet again to simply The Pigs.

Pilgrim's Bottle

At Linford, in Buckinghamshire, the Pilgrim's Bottle remembers the days when travellers stayed overnight at various religious houses en route to such shrines as the tomb of Thomas a Becket in Canterbury. Note this will not have been a glass bottle, for much of the history of the pub the bottle was made from leather and sealed by tar.

Pimlico Tram

Two distinctly different origins for the two words in this pub name. The latter is the easiest for the premises has long displayed memorabilia of the golden age of the trams, with an emphasis on local routes. When it comes to the district of Pimlico the place took the name of a family who once lived here, in particular Ben Pimlico who was landlord of the inn, one known for its own brew of nut brown ale. Thus the landlord gave his name to the pub and, thereafter, the area, quite the reverse of what normally happens.

Pipe and Gannex

Only one man fits both items, former British prime minister Harold Wilson. The only connection with the man is he was in office when the pub opened.

Plank, Hook and Shovel

There can be few more 'local' names in the country than this example where each refers to a feature in and around the premises. Until the middle of the 20th century, customers had to use the Plank to cross the dyke and gain access to the pub where they would see the Hook on the wall alongside the front door from which hung the Shovel – the latter being used to remove the horse manure which collected here while their owners were (where else?) in the pub!

Playhouse

As the name suggests this Colchester building opened as the Playhouse Theatre in 1929. Within five years it had become a cinema, then in 1981 the inevitable bingo hall.

Plough

A simplistic and common pub name where an actual plough, or a model of same, was used as the sign. Its message is simple, it says this establishment is open to anyone – the idea coming from a time when everyone earned their living from the land, be it directly or indirectly.

Plumpers

A definition that may have been created to explain the name but, with no other suggestion, we must point to the long-held belief this is a local term for a tall tale, something often heard within.

Podger

Is an unusual trade name or, more correctly, a tool employed by the nearby foundries. This enables large bolts to be tightened or loosened, effectively a large wrench.

Port Out and Starboard Home

An acronym that also happens to be the name by which the local Peterborough United Football Club are known. This is held to have been coined, albeit inadvertently, by former manager Pat Tirrel who demanded, "Posh football from a posh team." However, this has nothing to do with the origin of the word 'posh', itself thought to be a loan word possibly from Romani, although it certainly has nothing to do with the acronym.

Postchaise

Today we would expect to catch a bus at a bus stop and a train at a railway station. Travelling in the coaching days would mean waiting at inns named to show such would call there, names such as the Coach and Horses. Here the service carried no passengers and was solely for the mail. A chaise is a light two or four-wheeled vehicle built for speed, this from the French word for 'chair'.

Postgate

An odd name for a public house with an even more unusual story behind it. We know this refers to Nicholas Postgate of Egton in Yorkshire, a Catholic priest who lived in a time when anti-Catholic feeling seemed to have abated. Unfortunately, for Postgate the infamous Titus Oates created the Popish Plot in 1678, a supposed conspiracy aiming to place a Catholic on the throne. Nicholas Postgate was dragged into the affair and was one of the last to be executed for such 'crimes', the execution saw him hanged, disembowelled and quartered. In November 1987 Postgate was one of 85 Catholic martyrs beatified by Pope John Paul II.

Postilion

The name suggests this was once a coaching inn for a postilion was originally a messenger or post boy and, later, the driver of horse-drawn coach. However, the postilion did not sit on the coach but rode one of the team of horses. As a pair this would be the animal on the left or near side, all horses were trained to be mounted from the left only; this is also the reason the left-hand side of the vehicle in the United Kingdom is known as the 'near' side. When there were four horses either two postilions were used or, when just one was available, he would ride the rear of the two on the left as this enabled him to control all four. The postilion was no more a part of the coach and coachmen than the horses but considered a part of the 'team' and changed at the same places as the horses.

Pot o' Four

An interesting name that conveys two messages. Firstly, it is usually only found in areas where sheep are reared, for the 'pot' is a circular iron stove enabling four men to heat their wool-combing implements at the same time. There is another phrase, a Pot o' One, used to describe a misanthropic individual and thus four working so closely together suggests a friendly and sociable place.

Powder Monkey

A naval term for those who performed the dangerous task of filling armaments with gunpowder. Most often, these are said to be boys but this Exmouth pub remembers Nancy Perriam who served on board the *Crescent* and the *Orion*, who lived in nearby Tower Street until her death in 1865. Not that she had been a powder monkey for some time as, at the time of her death, she was 98 years of age.

Prince Arthur

At Fleet, in Hampshire, is the Prince Arthur, named for the building constructed in the 1890s when the nearby British Army camp at Aldershot came under the command of Prince Arthur, third son of Queen Victoria.

Prinny's

A pub named after the man who did much to bring the extravagant styles which typified Brighton in the Georgian era, the future George IV. However, when he influenced such as the Brighton Royal Pavilion he was Prince Regent, often referred to simply as Prinny.

Printer's Devil

Nothing to do with the power of the press, this expression pre-dates such great influence and refers to the errand boy common to every printer's office almost ever since the first presses were running.

Puffing Billy

At Torrington, in Devon, the station closed in 1965, although trains continued to run for another 17 years. All the station buildings survive, in particular those on the 'up' platform which became the Puffing Billy public house and restaurant. Tracks remain, where a coach, brake van and wagon stand, separated from the Tarka Trail, itself running along the old track bed, by a fence. Plans to relay the track to Bideford have been approved and continue to advance to the stage where short journeys behind a diesel locomotive will be possible.

Whilst the property is listed as a public house, it should probably be seen as a licensed restaurant. Inside, the walls are festooned with memorabilia examining the station in its heyday and around its closure. Just how the 'pub' came to be known as the Puffing Billy is unclear. One story speaks of the original licensee being a heavy smoker named William, although this is unconfirmed.

Puncheon Inn
For once the pub sign does define the name. The image featured is that of two men carrying a huge barrel, the puncheon, which holds at least 70 gallons.

Pyrotechnists Arms
Certainly a unique name, one adopted by the pub which served many an employee from the nearby fireworks factory. While the factory is long gone, the pub and its name survive.

Quicksilver Mail

A reminder of the London to Falmouth mail coach, which stopped at Yeovil where the pub of this name is found today. It achieved fame, and its nickname, by becoming the fastest long-distance mail service in the land including a record time of 16 hours and 34 minutes – this included changes of horses, Royal Mail business and three or four meals. This equates to an average speed of 10.25 miles per hour, which on roads that were little more than dirt tracks is not a journey any of us would be keen to endure.

Quiet Woman

This is not exactly as sexist as it seems, although today the image of a headless woman would be seen as such. At Leek, in Staffordshire, the image depicts a ghostly woman minus her head, with the unmistakable image of Henry VIII in the foreground. Clearly, this refers to the Tudor monarch's propensity for removing the head of as many of his wives as he bothered to divorce. Originally, the landlord who first coined such a name will have been searching for a way of speaking of a great rarity – a reference to the ales served within. This kind of cryptic message is common in pub names, indeed this same suggestion of a unique establishment is seen in the similar Silent Woman and the very different Black Swan.

Radjel Inn

Two pubs of this name in Cornwall, where the term is said to describe a loose pile of large rocks that provides a den for a fox. One of the pubs, that in Pendeen, saw one Willy Warren behind the bar for a laudable 59 years. His great-great-grandfather is said to have been nicknamed 'Radjel'.

Railway Tavern

Old branch lines serving smaller towns and villages invariably brought, and collected, passengers from a station located inconveniently outside the town. This resulted in a number of pubs being built near the station to welcome and offer refreshment to travellers. Such would be named for close proximity to the railway.

Ram Jam Inn

These premises on the Great North Road near Oakham in Rutland have a long history. It began as a coaching inn called the Winchelsea Arms later to change its name to the Ram Jam, although the real reason why is hidden among a plethora of tales and may never be known.

Of the many stories told there are a number of basic themes, including the most obvious that this was so popular an inn it was invariably 'ram jam' full. There is also the idea this was a liqueur brought to this country by a servant during the days of British rule in India. Unfortunately, the 'ram jam', a term for a manservant, never shared the recipe with anyone and its secret died with him, assuming it was ever a liqueur to begin with.

Yet the two most common stories concern a barrel of ale, although the telling differs depending upon who is telling it. There are claims that this was an early haunt of the infamous highwayman, Dick Turpin. It is claimed it was he who revealed the secret of drawing both mild ale and bitter from a single barrel. Taking a barrel he told the landlady to plug the hole he had just made for the mild with her thumb, he then made a second hole for the bitter and instructed her to plug this with her other thumb. He then heads off to search for the spiles to plug the holes. Of course she is now unable to move and never sees Turpin (or whomsoever the trickster is) again as he makes off without paying his bill and likely with the takings too. A variation on this story is told where it is the landlord who ends up with his digits in the barrel, whilst the wily conman turns his attentions to his buxom and attractive wife.

It does appear that some, if not all, of these explanations are rather contrived and it cannot be overlooked how the unique language used in pub names could well have created the name simply as a talking point. Indeed, the establishment released a supposed copy of an early explanation of the name detailing the 'thumbs in the barrel' story. However, it is interesting to note the copy does not give the original date.

Rann Wartha

A St Austell public house that recalls the earlier Cornish name for this area where rann wartha means 'the higher quarter'.

Rat

At Anick, in Northumberland, is as astonishing a pub name as is found anywhere in the country. This old drovers' inn was certainly here by the early 18th century and was known by its present name. Its history is well-documented although the name is a complete mystery. Of course, there are local explanations for the name. One suggests this was a meeting place for rat catchers, which hardly seems likely as how many rat catchers would a place the size of Anick require? Another tale tells this was where the largest rat ever found was caught, again this hardly seems plausible as, surely, no innkeeper would want to advertise vermin no matter how large. The third narrative tells how a landlord gave information to the officers of the Crown during the Jacobite uprisings of 1715 and 1745, earning the name 'The Rat'. This is the least plausible of the three for it is clearly a case of creative etymology.

Rattlebone Inn

This oddly-named inn is derived from the legendary local hero John Rattlebone. He is said to have been mortally wounded in a battle with the Danes and, despite heavy blood loss, applied pressure to his stomach wound with one hand and fought on alongside his colleagues until his last gasp.

Recruiting Sergeant

A reminder of the days when recruiting sergeants toured the land tempting local men to join the ranks when in the local pubs. Such a deal was sealed by the would-be soldier accepting the King's shilling. Many claimed the shilling was dropped into the tankard of men and, when they removed the coin having quaffed their ale, were said to have accepted it. It was around this time glass bottoms appeared in pewter tankards, was this the solution to the problem?

Red Alligator

Named after a racehorse, a bay gelding which won the 1968 Aintree Grand National with a starting price of 100 to 7. Ridden by Brian Fletcher, who at the time was only 19 years of age, and owned by Mr J. Manners, the choice of the pub name marked the trainer Denys Smith, whose farm could be found just outside nearby Bishop Auckland.

Red Lion

At its peak there were more pubs known as the Red Lion in England than any other. Numbers once exceeded 600 but in the 21st century this has fallen. For such a common name, the name has only been seen since the 17th century and, rather ironically, the most common pub name in England is representative of the monarchy of Scotland.

It began as a device on the coat of arms of the most powerful man in England in the 14th century, John of Gaunt. His vast riches would, in today's money, be worth in excess of £100 billion, making him one of the 20 wealthiest people in history. His successors went on to become kings of England through lines resulting in Henry IV and Henry

VII and, of course, their descendants. While few pub names can be traced to the 14th century and directly to John of Gaunt himself, his red lion symbol did come to England through a more circuitous route. Of his 15 named children, four with Katherine Swynford were later legitimised by royal decree, taking the surname Beaufort. Their descendants thereafter became every ruler in Scotland from 1437 and, following the accession of the House of Stuart in 1603, every monarch of England.

Reginald Mitchell
At Hanley, in Staffordshire, is this pub named after the local man who invented the Spitfire.

Resolution
Named after the flagship of Captain James Cook, the pub stands in Captain Cook Square in his home town of Middlesbrough.

Rhydspence Inn
A 14th century establishment at Whitney on Wye, in Herefordshire. This was an important meeting point for drovers on the Black Ox Trail, animals coming from as far afield as south and central Wales, and even southern Ireland, in order to take advantage of the better prices in the market places of the English economy. The name is a former place name, this being 'the rented fields of the bridges', with 'spence' a corruption of 'pence', also seen in the many nearby penny and halfpenny field names.

Richard John Blackler
This man founded the Blacklers department store which stood on this site in Liverpool.

Richmal Crompton
This pub in Bromley, Kent, remembers the author of the stories of the early life of William Brown. The author lived in Bromley for more than 20 years.

Roaring Donkey

In the resort of Clacton-on-Sea, Essex, we find the name Roaring Donkey, which must remember a particular animal. More often applied to a horse, the term 'roaring' describes an animal whose nasal passages are misshapen causing the animal to breathe noisily.

Robert Ransome

An Ipswich pub named after the man who established the nearby iron works here in 1789.

Rohan Kanhai

A pub in Ashington, Northumberland, for he appeared there when captain of the West Indies cricket team. Born Boxing Day 1935, Rohan Bholalall Kanhai was a batsman of great talent and consistency. His first three test matches, while touring England in 1957, saw him keep wicket and open the batting. However, it was as a middle order batsman he is remembered, his 79 tests seeing him average 47.53 with a career best of 256. Not that he was ever seen as a traditional test match cricketer – indeed his patient and steady half century in the inaugural World Cup final of 1975 was quite out of character, although it enabled Clive Lloyd's explosive hitting to build a match-winning total – some of his shots were most unorthodox, including the 'falling hook shot' which saw him end up on his back and the ball invariably hitting the boundary ropes. Kanhai also played county cricket for Warwickshire, alongside fellow West Indians Alvin Kallicharran, Derek Murray and Lance Gibbs. Behind England openers Dennis Amiss and John Jameson his 11,615 runs at an average of 51.62 made him the highest run scorer for the county, a record which was to last until the record books were rewritten by countryman Brian Lara.

Romper

The example of interest is found near Stockport, in Cheshire. A very grateful former landlord changed the name of his pub when he saw a substantial return on the wager he placed on a horse called Miss Romper.

Romping Cat

This is a variation on the Mad Cat, this example found at Bloxwich in the West Midlands. This establishment had been known as the Sandbank Tavern and showed a sign bearing the coat of arms of Sir Gilbert Wakering, the former lord of the manor. The heraldic image included a lion rampant or, as the locals knew it, the Romping Cat which was eventually used as the official name.

Rorty Crankle

A delightful name from Plaxtol, near Sevenoaks, in Kent, which is not only unique but reflects the locality, too. The village of Plaxtol's name means 'place of play', with 'rorty' a 19th century dialect word meaning to 'have a good time' a fitting choice for the local pub. The addition of 'crankle' is another dialect word meaning 'twisting' and refers to the location at the junction of two roads.

Rose Salterne

A Bideford establishment honouring the name of the heroine of the Charles Kingsley novel, *Westward Ho!*

Round Stone

A pub named after a local story in East Preston, West Sussex, a story portrayed on the pub sign. The body of a man who committed suicide was interred here at the crossroads, such deaths were not permitted a burial in consecrated ground. As it was thought these souls would never find rest, the fear of them coming back to haunt meant steps were taken to prevent them escaping their burial site. Here, not only was there a stake driven through the body, but that stake also passed through the hole in the centre of a heavy millstone, making it doubly difficult for the ghost to exact any revenge.

Royal Oak

One of the three most common pub names in England this was unheard of before the middle of the 17th century, for it remembers one of the best known narratives in the history of our islands. The oak tree in question is the Boscobel Oak, a large specimen in Shifnal, Shropshire, where Charles II and his aide, Colonel Carless, hid from noon to nightfall to escape the Parliamentarian soldiers. Following his defeat at the Battle of Worcester in 1651, King Charles was aided by a number of his supporters as he attempted to flee the country. After a number of close shaves, he was smuggled to France by members of the Pendrell family disguised as a woodman, complete with a severe haircut and stained face and arms to make it look as if he was used to working outside. Nine years later at the Restoration of the Monarchy, 29 May, the date of the king's birthday, being chosen as the official date, it was thereafter known as Royal Oak Day.

The present tree is not the original, this was destroyed by souvenir hunters in the 17th and 18th centuries who removed pieces of bark and even whole branches. A second tree, from an acorn of the first, known as the Son of the Royal Oak, grew until it was badly damaged by a storm in 2000. A third tree was planted as a sapling by Prince Charles in 2001, this had been grown from an acorn taken from the 'Son' and is thus 'the grandson'. Modern-day souvenir hunters can still acquire a piece of the history, for other grandchildren of the Boscobel Oak are on sale here. Buyers receive their small oak along with a certificate of authenticity.

Running Horses
At Mickleham, in Surrey, is a pub recalling the Epsom Derby of 1828. Two horses, named Cadland and The Colonel, could not be separated and the most prestigious flat race in Britain was declared a dead-heat. Remarkably the race was rerun and Cadland proved victorious, if only by a neck.

Rusty Axe
A local name with a unique, if rather disappointing, origin. Found on the Somerset levels, cutting the withy has been a traditional task since prehistoric times. One cutter was rather careless and left his axe behind and when it was found it was rather rusty, hence the name of the local pub.

Saladin

At Little Somerford, in Somerset, the sign does not feature the leader of the Muslim forces in the Crusades but a hot air balloon. In 1898 the MP for Malmesbury, Walter Powell, moved to Little Somerford and in three years did much for this village. He was a keen hot air balloonist and in 1888 was experimenting with his most prized possession, a balloon he had named Saladin, when he lost control and was last seen heading out across the English Channel, never to be heard of again.

Sally Port

The pub is in Portsmouth, although the term was once quite common to many ports around the country. The reference is to where boats were utilised to ferry crews to and from a vessel anchored offshore.

Sally Pussey's Inn

At Wootton Bassett, in Wiltshire, we find a pub name traceable to the latter half of the 19th century when the place was still known as the Wheat Sheaf Inn. At that time the licensee was one Sarah Purse, a woman who was held as faith healer to all living things. She stood just a shade over five feet in height, but had a presence and dominance over even her burliest customer – and was even said to have 'escorted' them from the premises on occasions without any trouble. She died in 1885 and is buried in the churchyard of Lydiard Tregoze, yet her legend lived on and, over the years, her name underwent changes, Sarah Purse became Sarah Puss, Sah Puss and, ultimately, Sally Pussey. In 1971, her pub was changed from the Wheat Sheaf Inn, to Sally Pussey's Inn.

Same Yet

The story of how this name came about seems a little contrived but, as there are no alternatives known, that version is given here.

It is said the name came about when the premises was still known as the Seven Stars and decorators came to repaint the exterior. When, in response to the question, "What colours?" the reply came, "Same yet!" (same again). The nickname stuck and later became officially adopted.

Samuel Lloyd

Corby in Northamptonshire grew rapidly following the opening of the iron and steelworks in the late 19th century. Samuel Lloyd being central to the town's development.

Saxon Shore

At Herne Bay we find a coastline which has seen more than its fair share of coastal defences since Saxon and even earlier Roman times. However, this name is not taken from any of these defences but from the Saxon Shore footpath which passes right in front of this pub,

Seahorse Inn

At Leysdown-on-Sea, in Kent, is the Seahorse Inn, clearly a maritime reference but not always to the very unfishlike creature known by that name. In early days, mariners referred to the walrus as a seahorse and there is a small chance this could have influenced this pub name.

Seven Red Roses

A lesson in naming a new pub was given when the local press ran a competition to name the pub on the new Lower Earley housing estate in Berkshire. Yet they did not simply ask for suggestions but asked three questions: favourite number, favourite colour and favourite flower. When counted the most popular answers were put together to produce Seven Red Roses. Sadly, soon after the pub opened the landlord died from heart problems. When his widow remarried the newlyweds emigrated to Florida where they are rumoured to have opened a new pub which they also named the Seven Red Roses, although no evidence has ever been discovered.

Seven Stones

A pub on the Isles of Scilly named after a group of rocks found 15 miles west of Land's End and seven miles east of the Isles of Scilly. Correctly, this is a reef two miles long and a mile wide. Over the years this has proven a danger to shipping, with 71 named wrecks and some 200 wrecks overall. Undoubtedly, the most famous was in March 1967, when the oil tanker Torrey Canyon broke its back on the rocks. The resulting oil spillage was, at the time, the costliest shipping disaster ever and remains the worst ever oil spill on the coastline of Britain. Since 1841 the reef has been protected by the Seven Stones light vessel.

Share and Coulter

At Herne, in Kent, is this excellent, and likely unique, variation on the common name of the plough, these being the two kinds of blades found on the plough.

Ship

A pub where the sign will often depict a seagoing ship, typically a large sailing vessel with two or three masts and a large area of sail and, when the establishment is near the coast or navigable river, this is quite possibly the origin. However, the majority of 'ships' are nowhere near sizable bodies of water, which has led to these being said to have been built using ship's timbers. Again this is more than possible as ship's timbers are simply those of a standard used to construct ships. This has not prevented the stories of how wrecked vessels have been taken apart and the huge timbers carried many miles inland to build an inn – such tales are not only implausible and impractical but quite laughable.

The most common origin for a 'Ship' inland is as a corruption of 'sheep', a reference to the wool trade and how many inns acted as warehousing for the massive distribution network in Britain. This network produced the wealth upon which Britain built its empire, an empire ironically enforced by the ships of its Royal Navy.

The Ship

THE SHIP

Ship in Distress

A pub named for the conflict off Hengistbury Head. Here, the story of smugglers and contraband, bravery and lovers begins with the *John and Susannah*, a vessel of 100 tons boasting 14 guns and under the command of Captain Coombs. Likely this vessel was as often considered a privateer as it was a smuggling ship, such changed their colours depending upon the nationality of the potential target. Coombs often paid a visit to the inn of a Mrs Payne, not only to partake of ale and a good meal but also to share her bed.

One day, he bade her to hold a package containing various documents relating to payment due from merchants and traders. Saying he would return and marry her, he left on, what would turn out to be, his last voyage. Her curiosity soon got the better of her and she rifled through the documents when she found a letter from a woman in Coombs' home port of Hamble. Therein, she read of her lover's promise to return to her and take her hand in marriage.

Probably within hours the revenue men had been informed of the expected arrival date of the *John and Susannah* and thus, when she rounded Hengistbury Head, the captain discovered he was staring down 20 barrels of the guns of HMS *Osprey*. Rather than fight, Coombs gathered every hand on deck and launched a terrific volley at the *Osprey*, killing its commander, Captain Allen, instantly. For three hours, the two vessels fought with the customs men eventually being victorious. All were captured but only Coombs faced trial, his crew were loaded on to a warship and enlisted in the coming battles against the French Navy culminating in Trafalgar.

Captain Coombs' guilt was unquestioned and his life ended by the hangman's noose. His body hanged on a gibbet at Stoney Point for a while, until parties unknown (almost certainly former smuggling associates) cut him down and took him home to Hamble where the local vicar was roused from his slumbers and made to give him a decent burial in the churchyard.

Short Blue

At Gorleston-on-Sea we see how mackerel fishing was an important industry operating out of this coast in the late 19th century. With over 200 vessels Hewitts were the largest company, their vessels flying a short blue flag and giving a name to the Short Blue public house.

Shrew Beshrewed

To understand this name we need to see how, despite the similarities between the two elements, these have quite different meanings. Whilst the first may still be understood as a reference to a scolding or nagging woman, the second is much more obscure in originally being 'beshrewed' or 'taken by the Devil'. Here the 'guilty' woman faced a ducking, courtesy of a chair suspended over the river.

Shroppie Fly

Not, as we would expect, in Shropshire but near Crewe in Cheshire. Here the reference is to the Shropshire Union Canal, the 'fly' being a boat which, by virtue of changing horses and crew, worked around the clock so as to deliver its perishable cargo.

Silent Woman

As we have already seen in names such as the Honest Lawyer and the Black Swan, many pubs are keen to advertise themselves as a rarity or even a unique establishment – the reference, of course, is to the product. Here the message is the same, despite these days of political correctness the humour in the name continues to be seen in the names of the Silent Woman, something the landlord considers almost impossible to find.

Sir Henry Tate

A Chorley, in Lancashire, establishment named after the town's favourite son. Sir Henry Tate started his working life as a grocer, later he made a large fortune through his sugar-refining business and his name is preserved in the most famous art collection in the land, held at the Tate Gallery.

Sir John Baker

A man who lived in Portsmouth near the pub which now bears his name. Twice Lord Mayor (1870 and 1875), he also served as the local MP, was a justice of the peace, chairman of the school board, offered employment as the owner of several shops, he was universally known as Honest John.

Sir John Barleycorn

Sir John Barleycorn was not a person but a humorous term for a beer or ale. Hardly, if ever, used today, 'he' is the subject of a folksong which humorously suggests that drink is the best friend of all and which says:

> Though the Hawthorn the pride of our hedges may be,
> And the rose our gardens adorn,
> Yet the flower that's sweetest and fairest to me,
> Is the bearded Barleycorn.

> Then hey for the Barleycorn,
> The Bonny Barleycorn,
> No grain or flower
> Has half the power
> Of the Bearded Barleycorn.

> Tho' the purple juice of the grape ne'er find
> Its way to the cup of horn,
> 'Tis little I care – for the draught to my mind,
> Is the blood of the Barleycorn.

> Then hey for the Barleycorn,
> The Bonny Barleycorn,
> No grain or flower
> Has half the power
> Of the Bearded Barleycorn.

> Tho' the Justice, the Parson and eke the Squire,
> May flout us and hold us in scorn,
> Our staunch boon friend, the best Knight in the shire,
> Is stout Sir John Barleycorn.

> Then hey for John Barleycorn,
> The merry John Barleycorn,
> Search round and about,
> What Knight's so stout
> As bold Sir John Barleycorn?

The name is also illustrated in the writings of Robert Burns, Sir Walter Scott and Nathaniel Hawthorne, although not always shown in the same light but seen as the demon drink.

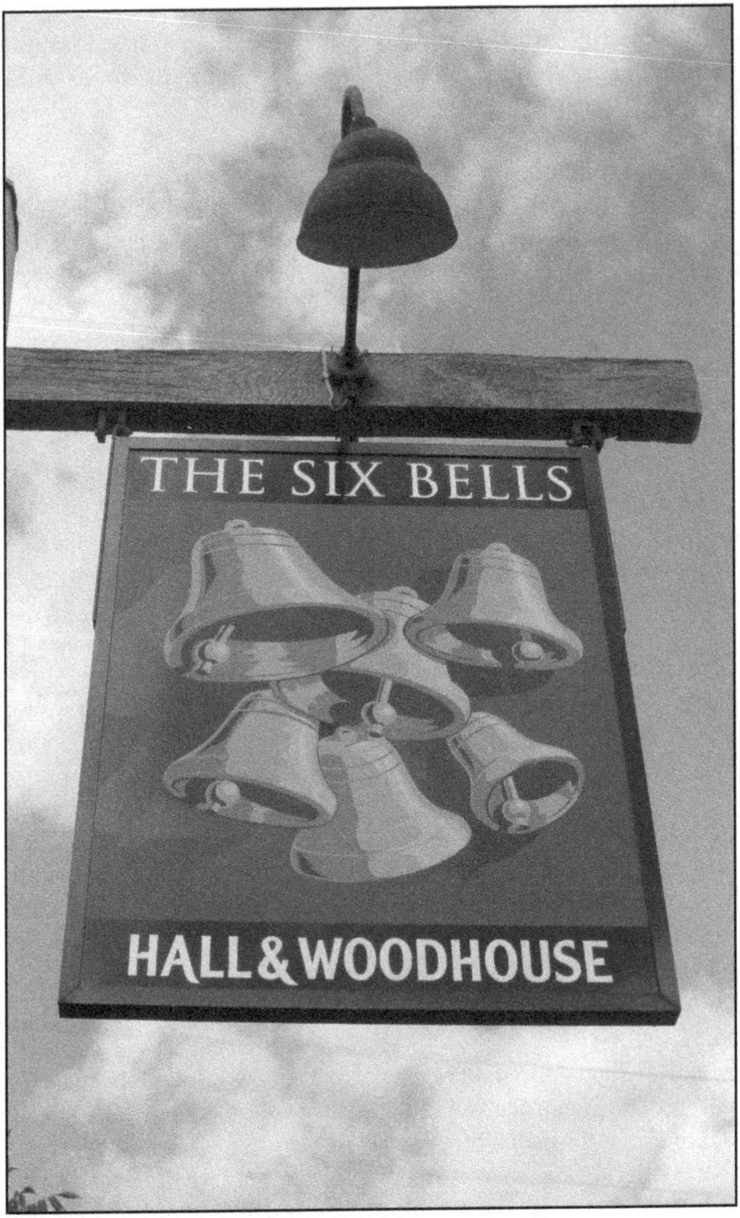
THE SIX BELLS
HALL & WOODHOUSE

Sir Julian Huxley

At Selsdon, in Surrey, is this pub commemorating a man who was instrumental in the creation of the Selsdon Wood Nature Reserve, he was also the first Director General of UNESCO.

Sir Michael Balcon

An Ealing pub taking the name of the man who helped produce many of the Classic Ealing Comedies, including *The Lavender Hill Mob*, *Passport to Pimlico*, and *Kind Hearts and Coronets*.

Sir Percy Florence Shelley

This is named after the man who lived at Boscombe Cottage near Bournemouth. As the son of the poet Percy Bysshe Shelley, his home later became a museum to his father's life and work.

Sir Richard Owen

In the county town of Lancaster is a pub named after the locally-born anatomist who will forever be remembered for his coining of the word 'dinosaur'.

Sir Thomas Gerard

Ashton-in-Makerfield's most famous family and, possibly, the best known of that family as he was imprisoned in the Tower of London having attempted to free Mary, Queen of Scots.

Six Bells

Originally, this was simply the Bells when first recorded as a pub in 1784. Soon afterwards it is found as the Five Bells, named for the number of bells in the church opposite. In 1805, the pub had to be renamed when an extra bell was hung in the belfry.

Six Lords

A name which commemorates the six peers who came through the village of Singleborough en route to their imprisonment in the Tower of London. All were guilty of having played some role in the Jacobite Rising of 1715, also known as Lord Mars' Revolt, when James Francis Edward Stuart, more often referred to as the Old Pretender, attempted to take the throne.

One of the six, William Maxwell, 5th Earl of Nithsdale, never made it to the scaffold and the executioner. On the night of 24 February 1716, the night before the scheduled execution, he managed to do what few have ever done, he escaped from the Tower of London. His wife was allowed to say her goodbyes to her husband and admitted to his room. In the gloom of the burning torches Maxwell exchanged clothes with his wife's maid and simply walked out the door with his wife. Together they fled the country, reaching Rome where they lived out the remainder of their lives.

Sixteen String Jack
This is not only the local pub but the nickname of John Rann, a highwayman in this area in the 18th century. He earned his name from the eight coloured strings he wore around each knee of his breeches, he being marked out by his love of fashionable clothing.

Six Templars
A pub in Herford named for the arrest of six men in Dinsley. All were members of the Knights Templar, correctly the Poor Fellow Soldiers of Jesus Christ and of the Temple of Solomon, at least four of them were held in Hertford Castle. A number of stories have been told of tunnels under Hertford where there lies evidence of the location of the Holy Grail.

Slab House
This was named for the stone slabs outside the city of Wells, in Somerset, where food was left for the residents during an outbreak of the plague in 1644.

Slug and Lettuce
When the majority of the population were illiterate, the image on the sign spoke volumes when the words were as unintelligible to most as hieroglyphics are today. However, commissioning a sign could prove prohibitively expensive, so the landlord or innkeeper would use a simple image and offer a few drinks to a regular in return for their artwork. In one example, the landlord asked for a rural scene to reflect its location and the sign was soon hanging outside. However,

the artist's skills were not as good as claimed and what was supposed to be a cow in a field looked more like a 'slug and lettuce'.

One of the earliest examples of the name comes from Stratford-upon-Avon. A double-sided sign, one shows the bed of lettuce with an unquestionably deliriously happy slug sitting on its meal. It must be added how, unfortunately, some 'slugs' are depicted as reminiscent of Brian from the *Magic Roundabout*, who of course was a snail and is shown complete with shell. The reverse of the sign showed a village cricket scene and the batsman having 'slugged' the cricket ball into a bowl of lettuce prepared for the tea interval.

Snuff Mill

A late 20th century pub that remembers a flour mill on roughly the same site. It was run by a man known as Snuffy Jack, who earned his nickname through his habit of taking snuff not, as was normal, from the back of hand but from his forearm.

Soldier Dick

A soldier who came here during the 16th century and was nursed back to health by the innkeeper's wife. When well again, he stayed on in the village, regaling the locals with stories of his adventures before he came to Furnace Vale.

Sospan Fach

What can only be a Welsh pub and a name inspired by the song of the same name. It translates to 'Little Saucepan' and is a traditional folk song associated with Llanelli Rugby Football Club. It tells the story of a harassed housewife and is linked to the rugby club through the town's tin plating industry – indeed, the goalposts were adorned with saucepans at both the club's old ground and the new.

Sovereign of the Seas

Named after the family who gave their name to Petts Wood in Kent. Phineas Pett designed the *Sovereign of the Seas* for Charles I – in its day the finest ship afloat.

Sow and Pigs

A pub in Toddington, Bedfordshire, with a name derived from a corruption of 'My Sow's Pigg'd', a card game played around the 17th century and one which has been forgotten save for the odd historical reference to the name.

Spectre

An ideal name for a pub in Pluckley, Kent, for this is reputedly the most haunted place in England, itself the ghost capital of the world, through having more reported ghosts per square mile than anywhere across the globe. Pluckley's claim is based on the number of reports against the population.

Spotted Dog

The image on the sign outside the Spotted Dog is clearly a Dalmatian. First bred in the eastern European area known as Dalmatia, hence the name, These dogs were first kept in Britain because they could keep up with a horse and trap, their spotted coats making a good contrast. Whether the dog is the true origin depends largely on the age of the establishment and its name, for the earliest are probably heraldic and thus not dogs but leopards.

Spyglass and Kettle

A Bournemouth pub with a created name, taken from two former pubs known as the Lord Nelson and the Steam Engine and suggesting the famous admiral was standing on the footplate of a locomotive.

Squinting Cat

A pub name in the same vein as the previously mentioned Drunken Duck. There are a handful of pubs of this name, all of which have a different variation of the haughty and/or aloof expression on the face of the pub cat. One example, at Clipstone in Nottinghamshire, was the winning entry in a 'paint a sign' competition. It pictures the pub's cat trying to focus having sampled the spilled contents from a leaking barrel.

Squire Knott

At Oldham we find this pub named in honour of a man who had his photographic studio on this site. A gallery of his images of Oldham is to be found nearby.

Standing Order

A Southampton pub which occupies the site of a bank, hence the name.

Stanley Jefferson

Bishop Auckland was the birthplace of Stanley Jefferson, where his parents ran the Theatre Royal. However, he later moved to America where he changed his stage name and earned worldwide fame as the first part of the double act Laurel and Hardy.

Startled Saint

At West Malling, in Kent, the nearby airfield of Biggin Hill saw many an RAF fighter scrambled during the Second World War and, in particular, during the Battle of Britain. The saint in question is St Leonard, a local individual who would have been very surprised by the small aircraft pictured circling his head.

Starving Rascal

One of the few pubs with a sign depicting a different image on each side, where the different images effectively point to 'Starving' on one side and 'Rascal' on the reverse. This unique name is quite recent, for until 1977 this was the Dudley Arms, although the story behind it comes from much earlier in the 20th century.

It is a cold winter's night and a tramp calls at the pub asking for shelter and some food. The landlord at the time was not in a charitable mood and showed the man the door. However, the man did not travel far, the pub stands on the corner at a road junction and he rounded the corner and slumped on the three steps leading up to the door giving access to the living quarters above. His lifeless, frozen body was found next morning. Yet this was not the last heard of this gentleman of the road, for a few years later strange things happened at the pub. At first his ghostly antics were, at most, a nuisance, yet before long both landlord and staff were being driven to distraction by the irritating behaviour of this apparition, whom they were convinced had returned to exact his revenge on the place.

Thus it was decided to rename the place in his honour in an attempt to appease him. The sign was changed, one side depicts a snowy scene with the landlord seeing the man on his way; the other shows the ghostly outline of the visitor raising a not-so-ghostly pint. Around the corner, next to the stone steps on which the body was found, is a plaque with a silhouette of the bent and dishevelled man with a walking stick. The legacy of the man lives on in the name of the pub which closed for a while and, since its reopening, has not had any reports of the ghostly visitor.

Steamer

At the top of a short, but fairly steep, incline in Welwyn, Hertfordshire stands the Steamer. Instantly, our minds turn to that quintessential image of the early industrial age, the steam locomotive. However, this incline is far too steep for any rail and, ironically, the term pre-dates the Industrial Revolution. Here the 'steamer' is a large and powerful horse, one stalled at the pub and hitched to the front of a team to help pull the cart up the incline.

Stewponey

Correctly, this should be the Stewponey and Foley Arms, for the family who made their fortune from iron. This pub near Stourbridge earned its first name when a British soldier came to run the pub after seeing action during the Peninsular Wars in Spain.

His military career now over, he brought with him his new wife, a Spanish woman born in Estepona. It was his intention to add the name of her place of birth to the sign but, as none of the locals were fluent Spanish speakers, it acquired the name of Stewponey.

Stone and Faggot

A seemingly strange name for a pub but a highly appropriate one considering this once housed the local bakery. Burning wood may produce heat but it is not controllable and temperatures fluctuate. Thus bakers would use the wooden faggots (bundles of sticks) to heat stones in the oven, these would stay hot for long enough to bake the bread by releasing the heat slowly.

Strawberry Special

The local at Draycott, in Somerset, tells its own story, featuring a GWR pannier tank engine hauling a truck of overly-large strawberries. This is a reminder that, before Lord Beeching got his hands on the Cheddar Valley line, fruit vans were a common sight along here. The pub was named the Strawberry Special to mark this line which closed in 1968.

Strugglers Inn

At Eagle, in Lincolnshire, is this unusual name today, yet the idea behind this such was quite common. Many will have seen the comedy image of the man wearing a barrel like an overcoat, allowing him some modesty. Puritan judges were fond of using such as a form of punishment, known as a drunkard's cloak. The same message was used in what seems a rather unusual advertisement on the leaflets and handbills produced by small businessmen and traders. Many will have seen, but probably not noticed, the image of the man with his head, arms and legs protruding from a globe. This is a plea for potential customers to use their services, an indication that the man was struggling through life, taking on everything the world had to throw at him. While today a businessman would emphasise his successes in order to attract trade, in the Georgian and Victorian eras customers were urged to spread their business and give everyone a fair chance. This name must have come from someone who employed this image to achieve the success which enabled him (or her) to have these premises.

Sugar Loaf

Also seen as Sugar Loaves and both instantly bring to mind the mountain at Rio de Janeiro, however, the loaf of sugar was known many years before. It was a wrapped conical package of sugar, similar to a giant ice-cream cone, and came to be used as the sign for a grocer. From the 17th century it was also used to represent a tavern.

Summoner

At Sittingbourne this pub is a reminder of Geoffrey Chaucer's *Canterbury Tales* where the Summoner is a character promising to tell us tales of others who were making the pilgrimage to Canterbury.

Sumpter Horse

A good name for a pub but one which is a little difficult to define as the use of the word 'sumpter' changed with the passing years. Originally, it referred to the driver of a pack-horse, then it came to mean the horse itself and, finally, the pack carried by the horse. Perhaps we should content ourselves with seeing this as advertising this place as where pack-horses, and more accurately the drivers, would regularly stop for refreshment, particularly in the days before the railways or even the canals made this ancient mode of conveying goods redundant.

Sun and Slipper

First recorded as an inn in 1642, when it was known as the Sun. This device found on the coat of arms of the Blount family. This coaching inn once offered a maintenance service for coaches, including changing the brake or 'slipper' which was soon added to the name. During the 20th century the name was changed to the Dog and Duck but, after a veritable outcry from patrons, quickly reverted to its original name.

Sun and Thirteen Cantons

An 18th century innkeeper hailing from Switzerland suggested this name as there were then 13 cantons (political regions of which there are almost twice as many today). This does not explain where the 'Sun' came from but is thought to have been the earlier name for the place.

Swan with Two Necks

A name which must be a sign painter's dream, these majestic birds most often shown with their necks forming a heart shape. However the name is nothing to do with romance, this is a corruption of Swan with Two Nicks, the Worshipful Company of Vintners being one of the few bodies allowed ownership of swans, other than royalty. Furthermore, the birds owned by the Vintners are marked by two nicks on the beak.

Sweyn Forkbeard

A name found at Gainsborough, in Lincolnshire, a reminder of the man who ruled much of Denmark, Norway and England by the time of his death on 3 February 1014 at the age of 53. His nickname, clearly which could not have existed before he was an adult, is rather ironically derived from the pitchfork-shaped moustache he wore in later years, a style he probably picked up from the English. Incidentally, if stuck for an original 'royal' pub name his father was Harald Bluetooth and his wife the rather oddly named Sigrid the Haughty.

Swyndlestock

A pub long gone but still commemorated in Oxford by a plaque. The pub itself was the venue for a bloody conflict between the townsfolk and those of the university – usually referred to as 'Town and Gown'. Some 60 students lost their lives on that day in 1355 but were apparently declared victorious. The name began as a variation on a term referring to the board used when dressing flax.

Tailor's Chalk
This building occupies 47 and 49 High Street, Sidcup, Kent. These had long been home to a cleaner's and dyer and that of a tailor, respectively.

Tame Otter
The river has also given a name to this pub near Tamworth, in Staffordshire. For a time this was known as the Chequers, although in recent years it has reverted to its original name of the Tame Otter. As expected the sign painter depicts the animal Lutra lutra, once hunted for its fur and in danger of extinction the European otter is now making a comeback. Inside the seemingly 'tame' otter is etched into every piece of glass, although here the image is that of the sea otter found off the coast of California.

Yet neither of these engaging creatures have given a name to the pub, the true origin is a simple rowing boat. Shallow, blunt-ended and for just one man, this particular vessel is rarely found away from the Trent and its tributaries. It is possible the boat, used by fishermen, was named from the water mammal but there is no evidence to confirm or refute this.

Tantivy
A unique pub name but one of the many linking the inn with the horse. This now obsolete word had two uses, one described the sound made by the hooves of the galloping horse while the other was heard during the hunt as the riders urged their mount on to its fastest gait.

Tap and Spile
An advertisement for the product is seen in the Tap and Spile, the two parts hammered into a wooden barrel to enable easy dispensing of the contents. The tap is clear, a very simple version of the modern

household tap, the spile is less obvious. Anyone who attempts to pour any liquid from a container will know if no allowance is made to allow air to enter and replace the volume of liquid drawn off causes a bubble to enter and the steady flow is interrupted, often with messy results. Hence the spile was hammered into the top of the barrel and removed to encourage a nice steady flow of the contents through the open tap, then replaced when the tap was closed.

Temeraire
Saffron Walden, in Essex, pays tribute to a name made famous by J M W Turner in his painting. However, this refers to a different vessel, the HMS *Temeraire* second only to HMS *Victory* at the Battle of Trafalgar. It was commanded by local man Sir Eliab Harvey.

Ten Bells
A name coined to refer, not to the number of bells in the belfry of the local church but, to the number of different churches whose bells can be heard from this establishment.

Thomas Botfield
The new town of Telford was transformed by this local industrialist.

Thomas Drummond
To give him his full name of Thomas Atkinson Drummond, here is the building that housed the Sunday School in Fleetwood. He is remembered for his role in providing cottages and churches for workers in the developing town.

Thomas Leaper
These premises in Derby used to be the Iron Gate House, previously the 17th century home of Thomas Leaper who is recorded as having to pay the hated hearth tax on no less than nine hearths – an indication of the size of his home.

Three Chimneys

Today there are quite clearly only two chimneys emerging through the roof but local tradition maintains the true origin is nowhere near so simplistic. During the Napoleonic Wars French prisoners were kept at a nearby camp. Being all officers their word was enough for them to be trusted to enjoy a walk outside the locked doors but were not allowed any further than where the three lanes converged (which is outside the pub). To the French this was les trois chemins which was misunderstood as 'the three chimneys' and not the correct translation of 'the three ways'.

Three Frogs

In these days when the term 'political correctness' has become a part of daily conversation, perhaps some knowledge of the origin and use of the word or phrase would make some realise it is not as insulting as they would have us believe. An example is found in the Three Frogs, a pub originally showing an image of three sheaves of barley (a brewing reference) but changed when a Belgian landlord arrived. When he added the delicacy of frogs legs to the menu he wanted to advertise it and where better than the name of the pub. It is common knowledge that 'frogs' was a term used to describe the French, always said to be due to their dietary preferences. In return, and for the same reason, the French refer to the English as 'roast beefs' as we apparently eat nothing else. However, this is quite wrong. Indeed the original 'frogs' were Parisians, named such by the other French people as the coat of arms of the French capital depicted, not frogs but, toads. Furthermore, it is likely this terminology for Parisians had been borrowed from earlier references to the Dutch, who had previously been known as 'Froggies' for reasons unknown. Hence it is not incorrect in a political sense but it is the understanding which is incorrect in this case and, we must wonder, in how many others?

Three Hats

In the case of this pub in Sittingbourne, Kent, we have a modern sign showing an image with three hats with plumes, much as those always depicted on the heads of Royalists during the Civil War era.

Previously, the sign showed a shako, a navy hat, and a billycock, as worn by a solider, a sailor and a businessman. Just what the message was is unclear but may well point to premises welcoming one and all.

Three-Legged Mare

A pub in the city of York known locally as the 'Wonkey Donkey'. Neither refer to an animal but are terms for a device of which a replica stands in the grounds. This is the name given to a gallows upon which three men could be hanged simultaneously.

Three Magnets

At Letchworth, in Hertfordshire, is this pub name that can be traced back to 1902 when Ebenezer Howard published a book entitled *To-Morrow: A Peaceful Path to Real Reform* outlining his idea of the garden cities. Howard's vision was of a town free of slums and enjoying the benefit of both town and country. The Three Magnets were the three directions in which the population would naturally be drawn: some to the town with its opportunities, amusement and good wages; others to the country to enjoy fresh air, good scenery and low rental properties; and those who wanted both in what he referred to as Town-Country.

Three Mariners

At Hythe, in Kent, the Three Mariners takes its name from a ballad by W. S. Gilbert. In 'The Yarn of the Nancy Bell' the mariner sings about being captain, cook, mate, bo'sun, midshipman and, indeed, the whole crew. His jolly song hides the awful truth, how after being shipwrecked this naval man only survived by eating his two colleagues.

Tibbie's Shiel's

Near Selkirk this pub recalls a long-serving 19th century landlady by the name of Isabella or Tibbie for short. She lived here at the 'Shiel' or 'shelter' until her 96th year and was known to several notaries including the writer Robert Louis Stevenson..

Tilly Whim

This comes from the name of a cave near Swanage, in Dorset. Local tradition maintains this was named from the local clay known as 'till' which could be moulded into any shape depending on one's 'whim'.

Tilted Barrel

At Sandwell, in the West Midlands, is a public house reflecting upon the subsidence in the area which has indeed produced a tilted building. While the sign depicts an individual taking advantage of the tilt to pour drink from the barrel, it is not just the container which is aslant.

Tim Bobbin

Urmston's John Collier was an 18th century dialect poet known as Tim Bobbin which was not only the main character in his works but also the poet's alias.

Tinker and Budget

At Oswaldtwistle, in Lancashire, is a pub name that is not as odd as it seems. While two random items linked by and or & are common enough in pub names, this example seems to be just random words. A tinker was a travelling metalworker, one who would repair or sell his handmade pots and pans. Here the link to a financial statement or proposal seems ludicrous, until we understand the origin of the word 'budget'. Originally, it referred to a bundle, or perhaps the contents of a bag, of documents. Later this was used to describe the bag which contained the papers, one made of leather was used by early Chancellors of the Exchequer, and thereafter to the modern use.

Tippling Philosopher

A pub in Sherbourne, in Dorset, recalling a former customer who is claimed to have walked the 300 yards to the pub and staggered the same distance home. Described as a natural philosopher, that is the explanation of science without real experimentation, Robert Boyle (1627-91) is best known as a scientist. Indeed, as any school pupil will know, he formulated what became known as Boyle's Law which relates to the volume, pressures and temperature of gases.

Tontine Hotel

Standing across the road from the first iron bridge in the world, which is of course at Ironbridge, in Shropshire, the name is also tied in to the bridge itself and represents another first, this time in the financial world.

This expression is derived from the name of Italian banker Lorenzo Tonti. He devised a method of investment and profit sharing that differed markedly from contemporary investment. Having raised sufficient monies by the selling of shares in the venture, the revenue raised was then shared between the investors at the end of each year. Normally, when the investor died his (or her) dividends were paid to the heirs, however, here the death of the investor marked the end of the contract and their share was split equally between the surviving investors. This continued until the last survivor, who until then received every penny in dividends, died and all future monies were retained.

Toss o' Coin

Some years ago this establishment, in Holmfirth, came under the auctioneer's hammer. It soon became apparent two bidders had offered the same amount and were not willing to increase their respective identical offers. An agreement was reached that the buyer would be decided by the toss of a coin and, when the place reopened, the name had, quite literally, been coined.

Towan Blystra

This pub remembers how Newquay, in Cornwall, was not known as such until 1439 when the Bishop of Exeter granted the change of name to New Key. Prior to this it had been known by its Cornish name of Tewynblustri meaning 'the blown sand dunes' and Anglicised to Towan Blystra.

Travellers Rest

A name echoing through history for the inn, indeed, the very sign itself, began as an advertisement to travellers that refreshment was on offer. This offer applied first to those on foot, later to passengers on the horse-drawn coaches, and was even used with the coming of the railways.

Travelling Hen

The local at Pontshill, in Herefordshire, was formerly known as the New Inn. A change of name suggested itself when one local hen decided to hop on to the rear axle of a lorry. The bird rode a little more than its luck until it was discovered some 30 miles away, still clinging on for dear life. Thankfully, the driver managed to rescue it and allowed her to make the return journey in the cab.

Treacle Mine

One of several pubs in the country that claim to have been built on the site of a treacle mine, this example being at Grays, in Essex. There seems to be a different geological explanation for every single example, and while those are speculative at best the creative versions are always more entertaining. The idea of the treacle mine came around the end of the 19th century, a time when coal was still the main source of power and thus it is no surprise to find a coal-themed explanation. It is said that prehistoric sugar cane had grown and become compressed, much as trees had produced coal so sugar cane produced treacle. A perfectly logical explanation as both were black! If not scientific, try historical and cite a notorious rogue. The ubiquitous Oliver Cromwell came and, for reasons unknown, buried several barrels of molasses. When the wood rotted the molasses seeped into the soil and the treacle mine was born.

Triple Plea

A visit to Halesworth, in Suffolk, will invariably mean a look at the pub's sign. For once, the image on the sign is not misleading, although the message is not overly clear. Here we see a man on his deathbed. Around him are three men: a lawyer, pleading for the man's estate; a doctor, interested in his body; and a clergyman, pleading for his soul.

Yet this is not the end of the story, for skulking at the back of the image is Satan himself, holding his badge of office, the three-pronged trident. The smile on the Devil's face shows the three are pleading in vain for he already knows the outcome. Just what this refers to is unknown, for there are no known traditional tales. Perhaps the message regards a former landlord or landowner. If so it is certainly not a compliment.

Trip to Jerusalem

To define this name we first need to examine the traditional explanation. It is said this place, in Nottingham, hollowed out of the very rock on which Nottingham Castle stands, was where Crusaders gathered before setting off for the Holy Land. This is based on two supposed 'clues' – the name, and the date painted on the outside of the building of AD1189.

It is recorded history how the first Nottingham Castle was erected in 1067, this a wooden construction. This was replaced by a stone building more than a century later. It is reasonable to assume the caves and tunnels underneath the castle, in what is known as Castle Rock and now houses the Trip to Jerusalem, began as storehouses for the castle. Furthermore, we can even concede these included a brewhouse serving the castle, yet this would never be a meeting place for knights and crusaders. Firstly, the ambience in such surroundings would hardly be welcoming for the nobility and, secondly, to gather in the centre of the country of an island nation for a trip overseas makes no sense whatsoever.

Records do not support this story either, for there is no record of any brewhouse here before the 17th century and no record of this name for a pub before the 18th century. The date of 1189 is also not relevant for the same reason. Furthermore, the English language shows this name cannot be from the 12th century as the word is not used before the 14th century and, even then, only to refer to a short journey and for pleasure. Neither applies to a crusade to the Holy Land.

Troll Cart

A reminder of the troll carts built to negotiate the narrow roads with the walls of the town of Great Yarmouth.

Trouble House

A strange name for pub when considering a pub's name and sign is intended to attract customers. Here the reference to problems are historical and four separate events could fit this name. Firstly, a Luddite uprising in the early 19th century, although the name may have pre-dated these problems but not the earliest conflict occurring when opposing sides in the English Civil War fought a minor battle nearby. Yet perhaps the name was coined when, during the intervening years, two later landlords committed suicide and thus suggests this name was unlucky.

Trumpet

The Trumpet at Bromyard, in Herefordshire, has also given its name to Trumpet Corner, the name being a reference to the warning for the coach's approach.

Try Again

A glance at the sign will show an image of an angler and the one that got away. However, this is a modern idea and the true origin comes from the problems when first trying to obtain a licence for the public house. As the saying goes "If at first you don't succeed..."

Tucker's Grave

A pub that takes its name from a minor place name, one now said to be a part of the car park. Mr Tucker was a man who lived in this village of Radstock until his death in 1747. As he had committed suicide in a nearby barn, he was not permitted a burial in consecrated ground. Hence his body was placed in this unmarked grave and the pub later took the name.

Twenty Churchwardens

Certainly a candidate for most creative pub name, and possibly one of the longest, is that of the Twenty Churchwardens. Surprisingly, this is a comparatively recent name, coined at the opening of the premises in 1968. Cockley Cley, in Norfolk, is one of ten villages comprising a church group. Those with a talent for mental arithmetic will have already guessed each has two churchwardens. All were invited to the opening night where 20 long-stemmed clay pipes were presented, quite relevant as these were known as 'churchwardens' in the 19th century, and an equal number of engraved tankards were set aside for each to enjoy a drink whenever they came here.

Twist and Cheese

A pub at Stondon, in Bedfordshire, advertises the popular fare of the ploughman's lunch, the cheese accompanied by a small loaf or roll baked from dough which had been twisted to give it a distinctive shape.

Twitchel

At Long Eaton a footpath connected the town with nearby Sawley, this footpath was known locally as the Twitchel.

Ugly Bug Inn

The Norfolk village of Colton was home to a large fruit farm until it closed in the 1970s, leaving a large barn. Built in 1810, the barn was looked at as a possible redevelopment project in 1982 by Peter and Sheila Crowland and their two children. When entering the premises the children noticed the old fruit baskets were still populated by some particularly gruesome looking invertebrates – which was why the eventual conversion was named Ugly Bug Hall and, when ten years later this found new life as a pub, became the Ugly Bug Inn.

Up Steps Inn

A modern Oldham pub taking a much earlier name for an inn. By 1805 the Nags Head had become the Up Steps as the entrance was above street level and thus the only way in was to walk up steps.

Vaga Tavern

A pub with only one known possible origin although it is impossible to see how it links to this corner of Herefordshire. Perino del Vaga was born Piero Buonaccorsi in 1501, an Italian painter of the latter Renaissance who learned at the side of Raphael. His mother died when he was just two months old and, with his father away fighting in the army of Charles VIII, was initially raised by his father's second wife. However, before his ninth birthday he was apprenticed to a druggist and then a succession of painters which eventually brought him to Rome and Raphael. Following the death of his mentor in 1520, he returned to Genoa where his own particular style blossomed and he painted his most memorable works. His work got him noticed and he returned to Rome where he was guaranteed a regular salary by Pope Paul III.

Van Dyck Forum

This has only been a public house since 1999, although the building was erected in 1926. The Van Dyke Cinema was built by W H Watkins, showing blockbusters for several decades until it became a bingo hall in 1973. The difference in spelling simply an error.

Vermuyden

A unique pub name is at Goole on the east coast. The Vermuyden named after Sir Cornelius Vermuyden. This Dutch engineer was brought to England by Charles I and knighted for his work in draining this region of the east coast in 1629 although he was not a citizen until four years later. His work proved extremely unpopular with the people, as his efforts were (at best) only partially successful. Draining the fen actually resulted in a drop in the levels caused by the drying of the peat, which had the reverse effect of bringing floods to other areas. After an enforced break for the Civil War he, together with some Dutch backers, succeeded in righting the problem with the digging of the Dutch River and brought the Ouse to the Humber at Goole.

Victoria

No woman has more public houses named after her than Queen Victoria. Not surprising considering she reigned for more than 60 years, ruling during a period of huge change and great leaps in technology and understanding.

Vigilance

Named after the last of the famous Brixham trawlers, *Vigilance* was originally launched in 1926, has now been restored and, once again, is moored in Brixham harbour where it can be seen from the pub.

Virginia Ash

At Henstridge, in Somerset, is a pub name representing, not a tree but, a story which unfolds on the sign. Here we see Sir Walter Raleigh, the man who sailed the Atlantic and landed at what is now known as Virginia, famously bringing back the potato and tobacco, hence the ash. Behind the famous explorer stands a man with a bucket of water, suggesting that maybe he was unsure if Raleigh was actually on fire.

V-Shed

A most unusual pub name but one reflecting the history of this Bristol building. At the beginning of the 20th century a number of transit sheds were erected at the city's docks. Identified by a unique letter, it is easy to see just where this unusual name originates.

Wallace Hartley

At Colne, in Lancashire, this pub, formerly home to a branch of the Co-Operative Society, remembers the local man who was bandmaster until his death in April 1912, his body returned to his home town where he was buried on 18 May that year. According to tradition it was he who continued to lead the players as the RMS *Titanic* slipped beneath the waves.

Waltzing Weasel

A Greater Manchester public house with a name referring to the weasel's propensity for dancing around its intended prey prior to pouncing. It is said this movement serves to hypnotise the target but this has no scientific basis.

War-Bill-in-Tun

At Warbleton, in East Sussex, is this pub named after the place, albeit only phonetically. The place name describes 'the farmstead of a woman called Waerburh', while the pub name uses 'tun' to refer to a large barrel and not the Old English tun or 'farmstead'. Here the 'War-Bill' uses the sharp implement used for cutting (compare 'billhook' today) with the addition pointing to a sword.

Ward Jackson

A Hartlepool pub that honours the man whose statue stands outside the premises. In 1844 he removed the first ceremonial spadeful of soil to begin construction of the coal dock of the Hartlepool West Harbour and Dock Company. As such he is regarded as the founder of modern Hartlepool.

Wash and Tope

Once this Hunstanton pub was named the Railway, of obvious derivation but quite ordinary and a competition produced an alternative suggestion of Wash and Tope. Firstly, it has two apparently unrelated elements connected by 'and', easily recognised as a pub name. Both parts are relevant to the area, the Wash is the large inlet between Norfolk and Lincolnshire and the Tope a species of shark caught in these waters.

Watercress Harry

This Kettering establishment was, rather predictably, named after a local man of some renown. He made his living by selling watercress in summer, moving to oranges, and wreaths made by his own hand in the winter. Whilst his appearance was unkempt, he is said to have been most polite, had no identifiable accent and was exceedingly erudite. It is rumoured he hailed from Leicestershire where he was disowned by his parents, in particular his clergyman father, when he took up prizefighting.

Water Poet

A Gloucester establishment remembering local man John Taylor. Born in 1580, he later moved to London where he worked as a waterman while writing his verse.

Westlegate

A Norwich pub, now named after the street, and originally called the Light Dragoon but popularly known as The Barking Dickey, because the badly painted sign looked more like a braying donkey than a horse and soldier.

West Station

As the pub name suggests this was once home to the West Station at Bexhill-on-Sea. Indeed, it was the terminus of the branch of the Hastings line. Aside from this watering hole, the building also houses an auction house, while the former track bed is home to a small industrial estate.

WEST STATION

Pub/Restaurant

Delicious Home Cooked Food
Traditional Sunday Roasts
Coffee and Snacks
Function Room Available

Telephone: 01424 222350

Wheel of Fortune

At Alpington, in Norfolk, is the Wheel of Fortune, which instantly brings to mind the television programme of that name but, of course, dates from much earlier. The phrase can be traced to both ancient Greek and Rome, where the goddess Fortuna was always depicted holding a ball or globe. In later years, this became a wheel, the circular form showing how the world keeps turning and bad luck cannot last forever or, conversely, good fortune is equally short lived.

Whiffler

Perhaps it was a previous job that gave the landlord the idea of naming this Norwich pub the Whiffler, for this man would walk ahead of the procession with his long pike-like ceremonial 'weapon' to clear the way for the main body coming behind.

Whistling Duck

At Banwell, in Somerset, is this, the winning entry in the local newspaper's competition to name the pub organised in 1967. This is an alternative name for the coot, held to be actively sought out by other wild fowl for their warning cry would alert them to danger from predators.

White Elephant

In modern parlance a 'white elephant' is something which proves not just worthless but a positive drain on resources. This is said to have originated in, what is now, Thailand but was once ruled by the kings of Siam. All-powerful rulers would make a gift of a white elephant to any courtier he disliked. It would be an unforgiveable insult to refuse and thus they were obliged to take care of the elephant without being allowed to recoup anything by putting the elephant to work, for white elephants are considered sacred in Siam/Thailand.

White Greyhound

At Edlington, in South Yorkshire, this animal was the constant companion of the First Viscount Molesworth, who erected a monument to the animal when it died. When walking the gardens of the estate one day the dog stopped his master from entering the privy by pulling on his coat tails. The master asked a gardener to investigate and the poor man was shot dead by a man hiding there, probably waiting to rob the house.

White Hart

This began as the heraldic symbol chosen by Richard II. Never the most popular of monarchs, it is impossible that this late 14th century king's symbol has maintained its popularity down the centuries and is still the fourth most popular pub name in the land.

It was not until the name became the generic term for all inns that the White Hart grew in popularity. If this seems unusual then consider the ubiquitous vacuum cleaner. Found in households the length and breadth of the land, technological improvements have seen many new innovations in recent years and yet, irrespective of the manufacturer, housewives still manage to refer to themselves as 'hoovering'.

White Rock

In defining the name of the White Rock public house at Underriver, in Kent, we likely discover a link to Wales. Here the Welsh folksong 'David of the White Rock' points to an early landlord being from the principality.

Who'd Have Thought It?

There seems to be a number of explanations for this name but two in Cornwall attract our attention, sharing the same origin. Both refer to the surprise (perhaps mocking) of the new landlord at being granted a licence to sell alcohol.

One of the most heart-warming stories of any pub in the land comes from Glastonbury. During the war servicemen and locals alike would while away their free hours at the Lamb Hotel. Years later, the son of a former owner returned to find the place in a most dilapidated condition. He and his wife enquired and, almost before they had drawn breath, had bought the place. The new landlord began extensive renovation, rebuilding a wall, replastering and buying new furniture before they could even open the doors for business. Then he turned his attention to the upstairs, new plumbing, more plastering and decorating, all the while never once mentioning the name of the place. Eventually, the place was restored to a standard which pleased the landlord and, standing back to admire the finished pub exclaimed, "Who would have thought it?" – from that day on the pub has been known as the Who'd A Thought It.

Whoop Hall

Carnforth in Lancashire's pubs include this local name for, what was once, the manor house known as Upp Hall. The name developed through the lord of the manor's love of hunting, and the hounds of his kennels, and was used as soon as the place was opened as licensed premises.

Wibbas Down Inn

A Wimbledon establishment that is named to remember the meaning of the place name of Wimbledon.

Widow's Son

At Bow is this most interesting pub name for it tells a story. In 1824, the pub was named for a widow grieving for the loss of her son who disappeared on his maiden sea voyage. However, she refused to give up hope and every year baked a hot cross bun for him on Good Friday. When she died it was discovered she had threaded these on a string and hung them inside her cottage. These were suitably passed to the pub where successive landlords have continued to add a single hot cross bun every year.

Wig and Fidgett

A pub in Boxted, Essex, with a truly wondrous name derived from it once being the site of the circuit court. This not only explains the 'wig' but also the 'fidgett', the name for the wooden stand on which the wigs were hung while not in use.

Wild Man

In the Wild Man we have a story that dates back to 1724 and the woods of Hanover. Here a boy was discovered and attracted the interest of George I. Peter walked on all fours, was unable to speak a word and ate the vegetarian diet of the forest. The king brought him to England and, when George died in 1727, his care was seen to by the Princess of Wales, Caroline of Ansbach. Peter became linked to Norwich in 1751 when he escaped from his care. When a fire broke out at the local bridewell the inmates were released. One very strong, and excessively hairy, individual turned out to be Peter. He was subsequently returned to his confinement in Hertfordshire and forced to wear an identifying leather collar for the rest of his life. This came in 1785, 61 years after his discovery and during that time he never learned to speak, read or write a single word. Many stories have been told of his birth and queries raised as to his parentage. Three centuries later the mystery of Peter the Wild Man remains as mysterious.

Wild Rover

An Irish traditional song entitled 'The Wild Rover' gave its name to the pub at Chesham, in Buckinghamshire. A sign depicts a man resting on his journey and enjoying refreshment. The man is dressed in a kilt and tam o'shanter, while the destinations on the signpost behind him are also erroneously Scottish towns.

William Aylmer

The present building in Harlow, Essex, was built in 1958 as Aylmer House. Taking the name of the family who lived at Moor Hall, the Aylmer family can be traced back to 1383 when the earliest recording was of one William Aylmer.

William Jameson

At Sunderland we remember the man who developed the area around Fawcett Street where the pub stands today.

William Robert Loosley

This pub occupies the former premises of a company founded in 1860, in High Wycombe, by the named carpenter and builder. By 1894, he had joined forces with a businessman named Pearce and, ten years later, a Mr Hull had also joined. Together they were cabinet-makers, builders, shop-fitters, undertakers, furnishers and gents' outfitters who continued to operate out of here until 1990.

William Stead

Darlington's pub is named after the man who wrote several articles for the *Northern Echo* before, in 1871, he was offered the job of editor despite having no other journalistic experience. He held the job for nine years, eventually dying in 1912, one of those who lost their lives aboard the ill-fated RMS *Titanic*.

Willow Walk

At what is now Victoria in London, this road was originally the causeway giving access to Westminster Abbey. By the Georgian era this had been planted with trees to give it the name of Willow Walk.

Windlesora

Many pubs feature the place name and it makes sense, for even if this is only representative of the street name it does show the location – an important consideration if the owners hope to attract business from farther afield. While this can lead to seemingly unimaginative names, here the owners have used the original Old English or Saxon form of the name of Windsor, where the Windlesora is located. This shows the origin of the place name as 'winding gear on a bank'. Here that is the riverbank where, in the absence of a landing stage or quayside, it was possible to wind goods on sleds, or similar, up the bank for unloading. It would be interesting to see the reaction of those who installed this functional technology when they learned their windlass had given a name to the royal family 1,500 years in the future.

Witch and Wardrobe

This Lincoln pub takes its name from one of the most famous children's books ever published, *The Lion, the Witch and the Wardrobe* by Clive Staples Lewis was published in 1950.

Woodrow Wilson

The 28th President of the United States has his name on a Carlisle public house as it was here his mother, Janet Woodrow, was born in 1826.

World's Wonder

Outside this pub in Warehorne, Kent, the sign painter has used his imagination to depict a cockerel having laid a square egg, which is hatching to reveal a bottle of beer within. The real origin is probably an even better story. In the middle of the 19th century two empty, and very run down, cottages were bought by local man Tom Night. Not known as a man of great means everyone wondered where he had got the money and, before long, with Tom working every spare minute on his investment, he was the talk of the village. At first, Tom ignored the chatter but, eventually, tired of the incessant gossip, turned on his neighbours and yelled: "You wonder where I got the money? You all wonder what is being built? Everyone wonders how I got the licence? Now the world wonders what Tom is going to call it? Well the world can stop wondering for there can be no more apt name than the World's Wonder!"

Wouldhave

A South Shields pub named after William Wouldhave, an 18th century boat builder whose work led to the development of the self-righting lifeboat.

Wounded Soldier

A Devon pub that has raised much money for military charities, although this is not the reason for the name. During the Second World War this was held by the landlady while her husband was serving king and country. He returned home alive after being badly wounded.

Wrong 'Un

England's national summer sport (cricket) gave a name to this delightfully named Kent public house. This refers to a delivery from a right hand leg spinner, which is released in such a manner that it turns the opposite way to his (or her) standard ball – ie turning to the leg side (for a right hand batsman) rather than to the off side. The correct term is the 'googly', although in Australia it is known as the 'bosie' after its creator, Bernard Bosanquet. If the surname sounds familiar it is probably down to his even better known son, Reginald Bosanquet among the most popular newsreaders of his day.

Ye Olde Bell and Steelyard

In Woodbridge, Suffolk, we find a name having two relevant elements, which may seem like stating the obvious but with pub names that 'and' is not always used as we would expect. Here the 'Bell' shows this was on church land, while the Steelyard is a simple device which is the forerunner of the modern weighbridge. It was installed around 1680 to impose tolls on loads exceeding 2.1/2 tons passing along the road and did so until as recently as 1897, when the technology was taken to London for an exhibition. Travel was also in mind when landlords offered rest and refreshment to both the traveller and his mount.

Bibliography

A Dictionary of Pub Names - Leslie Dunkling and Gordon Wright
Black Country Ghosts - Anthony Poulton-Smith
Cambridgeshire Place Names - Anthony Poulton-Smith
East Kent Place Names - Anthony Poulton-Smith
Haunted Worcestershire - Anthony Poulton-Smith
Herefordshire Place Names - Anthony Poulton-Smith
Lancashire Place Names - Anthony Poulton-Smith
Leicestershire and Rutland Place Names - Anthony Poulton-Smith
Norfolk Place Names - Anthony Poulton-Smith
Northamptonshire Place Names - Anthony Poulton-Smith
Northumberland Place Names - Anthony Poulton-Smith
Oxfordshire Place Names - Anthony Poulton-Smith
Suffolk Place Names - Anthony Poulton-Smith